THE BAFFLED PARENT'S GUIDE TO GREAT BASEBALL DRILLS

Jim Garland

Ragged Mountain Press/McGraw-Hill

Camden, Maine • New York • Chicago • San Francisco • Lisbon • London
Madrid • Mexico City • Milan • New Delhi • San Juan • Seoul • Singapore
Sydney • Toronto

To my dad, Calvin Garland, who was never too busy or too tired to spend time playing baseball with his sons.

Ragged Mountain Press 
A Division of The **McGraw-Hill** *Companies*

10 9 8 7 6 5 4 3 2

Library of Congress Cataloging-in-Publication Data
Garland, Jim, 1948–
The baffled parent's guide to great baseball drills / Jim Garland.
p. cm.—(The baffled parent's guides)
Includes index.
ISBN 0-07-138407-3
1. Baseball for children—Training. 2. Baseball for children—Coaching. I. Title. II. Series.
GV880.4.G37 2002
796.357'07'7—dc21 2001007477

Questions regarding the content of this book should be addressed to
Ragged Mountain Press
P.O. Box 220
Camden, ME 04843
www.raggedmountainpress.com

Questions regarding the ordering of this book should be addressed to
The McGraw-Hill Companies
Customer Service Department
P.O. Box 547
Blacklick, OH 43004
Retail customers: 1-800-262-4729
Bookstores: 1-800-722-4726

This book is printed on 70-lb. Citation by R.R. Donnelley & Sons, Crawfordsville, IN
Design by Carol Gillette
Production by Shannon Swanson and Dan Kirchoff
Illustrations by Debra Garland
Photography by Jim Garland
Edited by Jon Eaton and Shana Harrington

Contents

Small-group work offers lots of opportunities for one-on-one instruction.

Introduction

Great Baseball Drills: The Baffled Parent's Guide is designed to help both the beginning and the experienced baseball coach of players ages 6 to 13. As you prepare for the season, questions regarding creating a positive atmosphere, involving players and parents, organizing practices, teaching skills, and keeping kids' attention will arise. This book will help you address these needs so that you and your team will have a successful season. By "successful," I am not talking about winning. Having a successful season means providing a positive experience for the players while you help improve the quality of their play.

Most of my teaching over the last thirty years has involved the use of small-group activities that are fun and action-packed. This small-group format is highly motivating for the players while they develop the skills necessary for participation in game situations. Many of the activities found in this book reflect this philosophy. Many of the drills can be treated in any one of three ways:

- by breaking the team down into several smaller groups, with each group participating in the same drill
- as part of station work, with each group participating in a different drill
- by being modified to meet the individual needs of your players and your team as a whole

Some of the drills are confined to marked-off spaces called *grids*. Grids are designed to restrict the amount of space used for the drill. They help organize practice spaces and improve safety by reducing collisions or players being struck by balls hit or thrown by teammates who are working too close to each other.

How to Use This Book

This book is both a stand-alone collection of drills to improve your coaching and a companion volume to *Coaching Youth Baseball: The Baffled Parent's Guide* (Bill Thurston). *Coaching Youth Baseball* is the beginning youth coach's foundation, offering counsel on encouraging and motivating youngsters, dealing with parents, managing games, and, in short, providing a successful, rewarding experience for kids. *Great Baseball Drills* continues in the same vein but is more focused on skill building than on the myriad other facets of teaching and coaching that a beginning coach needs to learn. This closer focus permits us to include more drills in this book than you'll find in *Coaching Youth Baseball*. Either book stands alone; together they make an unbeatable combination.

The first two chapters include suggestions for creating an atmosphere of good habits and organizing practices and discusses such aspects as pro-

A successful season means providing a positive experience for all players.

moting teamwork, involving parents, improving basic skills, and winning and losing. In addition, tips on how to organize practice schedules, conduct productive practices, keep kids' attention during practice, and manage time appropriately are included. You'll also find suggestions for equipment for your team. Chapter 2 also offers the Ten Commandments of Practices to make your practices more rewarding.

The remaining seven chapters present drills to develop the skills of throwing, fielding in general, fielding by position, hitting, bunting, and baserunning. These drills are designed in a mostly small-group format, in which players benefit by getting lots of chances. The drills are presented for beginning (ages 6 to 8), intermediate (ages 9 and 10), or advanced (ages 11 to 13) players. Each drill includes a discussion of points to emphasize. Chapter 9 suggests a few "lead-up games" that I have found over the years provide lots of fun for beginning and intermediate players. These games simulate real game conditions but are modified to make them safe and rewarding for young players who are not yet confident fielders.

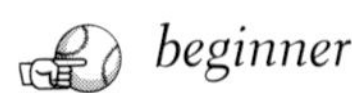

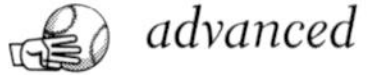

I hope the activities and suggestions presented in this book are helpful. I know the players will appreciate your efforts in allowing them to have fun while they're learning. They'll also appreciate the small-group approach as offered through these activities because they'll be engaged in playing instead of standing, watching, and awaiting a turn.

CHAPTER 1

Creating an Atmosphere of Good Habits

Promoting Teamwork and a Positive Environment

I was lucky to grow up in a neighborhood full of kids. We congregated mostly at my house because the baseball field was behind it. OK, it wasn't really a baseball field: it was an abandoned five-acre housing construction site sliced out of a forest.

We made dugouts, a backstop, and a home run fence. We even had a flagpole. We couldn't afford to line the field with lime, so we used black dirt we dug out of the forest. I bet ours was the only field around with black baselines.

What great memories. It seemed like we played all day long. Our best games were when a guy called Mr. Calvin would play. Mr. Calvin was the father of three boys in the neighborhood. He loved to play with all of the kids. He was the all-time pitcher, which meant we spent most of our time hitting and fielding and less time waiting for someone to throw a strike. The neighborhood kids loved Mr. Calvin. They couldn't wait for him to get home from work. I think they loved Mr. Calvin because he was always so encouraging, so positive, and always able to make them feel good about themselves. They also loved him because he was always coming up with ways to change the game that made it fun and full of action. I loved him for another reason: he was my dad.

Things have changed a lot since then. Houses have been built over the ball field, and Mr. Calvin has passed on. But what hasn't changed is that kids still love the game of baseball, still want to have fun playing, and still want action-filled activities. This drill book is the answer: it emphasizes action, technique, and participation by all players.

Your most important task as a coach will be to create team unity. While keeping the players active and helping to develop their skills, you will realize that each one is an individual, with different interests, needs, and abilities. It's important that you recognize and appreciate these differences while helping the players work cooperatively.

The best way to develop a cooperative spirit is to promote a positive atmosphere—in part by emphasizing player improvement and not comparing players to other players. Having consistent expectations for each player on the team—not a double standard for the star players—also promotes a positive atmosphere. Much of creating an atmosphere of good habits is the result of positive energy and reinforcement modeled by the coach during practices and games. An enthusiastic coach who designs fun practices, involves parents and players in decision making, and is supportive rather than dictatorial will discover that success is right around the corner. Promoting a positive atmosphere means you and your players should respect the rights and property of others, have the courage to make mistakes, be honest with yourselves and others, be responsible, and do the little things right. Have the players take ownership by making them responsible for their own equipment, uniforms, and other tasks that develop as the season continues.

Be sure to observe and make corrections to improve player performance. Do this in such a way that players don't feel threatened or put on display in front of the other players. Try a "catching-them-being-good" approach. Such positive reinforcement and feedback will go a long way in increasing players' willpower to engage in activities that stretch their ability levels. Players who are comfortable knowing that it's OK to make mistakes are less likely to be inhibited about participating. Don't tolerate criticism of players' performances by other players. Instead, promote encouraging words from teammates to help create a positive environment.

Coaches can do other things to promote a positive environment, including such simple acts as learning players' names quickly and being a good listener when players are sharing thoughts and concerns.

Involving Parents and Players

To have a successful team, you need a successful organization. Parents are an integral part of the organization. Just as players differ in needs and abilities, so do their parents. I have found over the years that the best way to get parents involved in the organization is to request their attendance at a team meeting before the start of the season. At this meeting, the coach—acting as a facilitator—begins a discussion about establishing team goals. Using input from the coach, parents, and players to establish team goals and policies gives ownership to all stakeholders involved in the organization. Empowering parents and players in decision making builds a sense of trust and ensures that everyone involved shares the same vision of the team.

Roles must be clearly defined in this process. Coaches should be good listeners and value input from others, but certain decisions, such as who will pitch the next game, belong only to the coaches. Coaches can use the information gathered at the initial team meeting concerning players' and parents' expectations to develop individual and team goals. For example, some players might want to improve their ability to catch ground balls. More skilled players may want to improve their footwork when turning a double play at second base. That's where the drills come in. They are designed to meet the needs of players at all levels.

Parents may be needed to fill other needs, such as procuring equipment, maintaining the field, and raising funds. Coaches may find that parent volunteers are more willing to continue with their support if they feel appreciated. Tell the parents when they have done a good job. A little recognition goes a long way. That goes for players as well. Praising good performance helps develop a culture of good habits. Communication between coaches and parents is essential for success. Establishing phone trees for emergency situations is helpful. Routine information might best be handled through a parent newsletter distributed on a weekly or biweekly schedule.

Give players lots of opportunities to improve fundamental skills, such as throwing.

Improving Basic Skills

Players learn by modeling, interacting, repeating, and synthesizing. They are motivated by a fast-paced, active learning environment and their intrinsic love of play—the basis for the drills developed for this book. Players will be motivated if they are involved in small-group activities with lots of variety and action while developing their skills.

Skills can be divided into two basic categories: physical ability and tactical judgment. Under physical ability are the actual skills of throwing, fielding, hitting, and baserunning. Tactical judgment is the ability of players to think on their feet and respond to the action around them. As players have the opportunity for numerous repetitions provided in the small-group format, their skills improve. As players begin to improve, they feel a sense of achievement. Positive reinforcement from coaches and teammates helps sustain their efforts. As each player's skills and judgment improve individually, the players become better collectively and approach practices and games with a more positive attitude concerning themselves and others. Success builds success.

Before each game, discuss with players defensive and offensive goals for that day. Defensive goals might include pitchers not walking more than one batter per inning, outfielders hitting their cut-off player on each extra-base hit, or catchers backing up first base on ground balls hit to the infield without runners on base. Offensive goals might include swinging at balls in the strike zone only, stepping out of the batter's box on each pitch to receive the coach's signal, or knowing when it's one's turn to hit.

Just like after practices, have postgame discussions where you address these goals with the players to see if they were met. Instead of emphasizing winning or losing, concentrate on the goals established by the team. Players' input in discussing what worked, what didn't work, and what to do about it is a valuable learning experience for everyone involved. This discussion is also the catalyst for developing goals for the next practice session and the next game. Through this process, players can constantly self-assess and reflect, asking, "Where am I concerning my skill level, where do I want to be, and how can I get there?" The emphasis should always be on improving individual skills, improving teamwork, and having fun—not on winning.

Coaches who emphasize winning as a way of being successful set their teams up for failure at least half the time. Players should not be exposed to a failure rate of 50 percent. Shifting an emphasis from winning to accomplishing clearly defined goals promotes a positive atmosphere for the players. It also helps you approach the game with more intelligence and less emotion. Remember, your players will very likely model your behavior. Be enthusiastic about the things you can control, and be even-tempered about the things you can't control, such as a bad call by an umpire. Your players will have a more positive experience and will be better able to enjoy the game and each other.

Meeting Equipment Needs

Equipment needs for playing baseball can be broken down into three categories: individual, league, and team. Each player on the team should provide his own glove and shoes. A shoe with molded rubber cleats is recommended for intermediate and advanced players. For beginning players, athletic footwear, such as tennis shoes, will suffice. Boys should also have athletic supporters and cups.

The basic equipment necessities for teams are often provided by the league. Teams of 6- to 8-year-olds require two dozen *safety balls* (balls that are lighter in weight with a softer cover to prevent injury). There are several types on the market, including sponge, hollow core with a vinyl cover, and foam with a nylon cover. Of these, I prefer the foam with a nylon cover because it has the size and similar weight of a baseball but its flight is restricted. Three or four bats of varying size and weight should be provided as well as six helmets of varying size, an adjustable batting tee, bases, and a home plate. Depending on the league rules concerning pitching at this level, a pitcher's rubber and catcher's equipment may also be necessary.

For teams of 9- to 13-year-olds, equipment should include three or four bats of different sizes, two dozen baseballs, six helmets of varying sizes, equipment bags, and catcher's equipment, including a chest protector, a

Baseball Safety

Safety concerns are addressed throughout this book. The Ten Commandments of Practices section in chapter 2 discusses the more obvious ones. You also can take other, less obvious safety measures through what you teach, how you implement the instruction, and what equipment you use to further ensure player safety. Here are a few suggestions.

Teach How To

- cross the midline of the body to catch
- position the glove for catching a ball
- avoid being hit by a pitched ball
- swing and hold onto the bat
- return to a base looking toward the outfield on a pickoff attempt
- position the top hand for bunting
- deal with the sun while catching fly balls
- communicate with teammates to avoid collisions
- protect the throwing hand of the catcher
- cover the bases properly
- warm up properly

Implement Instruction Using Procedures That

- use multiple stations that are spaced properly
- use *safety bases* placed a safe distance from anyone using a bat when performing station work (a safety base is a base placed 25 to 30 feet away from a batter, where the waiting players stand; this is instead of a backstop)
- use *grids* (areas identified using game markers) that are properly spaced
- never have players warming up while throwing toward the bench
- never have balls lying in front of the mound during batting practice
- never allow a batting practice pitcher to throw a pitch until a fielder has caught a fly ball hit on the previous pitch
- never allow a batting practice pitcher to throw a pitch while a fungo hitter is hitting to an infielder or while an infielder is throwing to a base—these things are accomplished between pitches
- never have infielders turned to the outfield to receive a ball while a ball is being pitched
- never allow players to take practice swings near the bench: designate bat swinging areas

Equipment Used Should Be

- modified to meet players' needs (appropriate size of bats and helmets, use of safety balls for beginners, etc.)
- checked daily for repairs (e.g., grips on bats, lacing in gloves)

face mask, a helmet, and shin guards. Other equipment usually furnished by the league at this level includes the home plate, pitching rubber, bases, a field liner, and occasionally safety nets. Uniforms differ from league to league but are generally provided by the league.

In addition to the standard equipment issued by the league, teams may want to supplement their inventory to better meet the needs of the players involved. For the beginning level, the added equipment might include *game spots* (circular pieces of colored rubber used to identify a space), *game markers* (cone-shaped, plastic or rubber pieces of equipment used to designate boundaries), scarves (used for developing eye-hand coordination when crossing the midline), whiffle balls, whiffle bats, whiffle fat bats, fleece balls, and a Hit-N-Stik (a piece of equipment that looks like a ball attached to a pole and is used to improve eye-hand coordination for batting).

For intermediate and advanced teams, whiffle balls, whiffle ball bats, batting tees, tennis balls, tennis rackets (which make hitting high fly balls much easier), safety balls, fungo bats, and a Hit-N-Stik can supplement the regular league inventory. An approximate price list for equipment follows.

- bat (metal) $25
- bases $10
- batting tee $25
- baseball $4
- chest protector $21
- face masks $15
- fleece ball $2.50
- fungo bat $25
- game marker $1.75
- game spot $2
- glove $35
- helmet $15
- Hit-N-Stik $40
- home plate $16
- safety net $110
- safety ball $4.50
- scarf $1
- shoes $25
- shin guards $20
- tennis ball $1.50
- tennis racket $13
- whiffle ball $1
- whiffle bat $5.50
- whiffle fat bat $5.50

Money used to purchase the equipment provided by the league usually is generated from registration fees paid by the players. Part of these fees should also go toward providing gloves and shoes to players who can't afford them. Any additional money needed can be derived from community sponsors, donations, and fund-raisers. To help limit costs, leagues can store equipment centrally so that more than one team can use the same equipment on different nights. Teams and leagues also should build their inventories over several years rather than purchasing all of the supplemental equipment during one season.

CHAPTER 2

Organizing Practices

Practice Schedules

You may be locked into practice times and game schedules provided by your league. If there is room for flexibility, ask parents what practice times suit them. Some days may be better than others. A reasonable schedule is two practices and one game per week. Coming to practice less than twice a week can make it difficult for kids to learn and remember the skills they are working on, and more than this can create time-commitment problems for families of primary and middle school students. Either way, have the schedules available at the first team meeting or practice so that every parent has a copy and knows what kind of commitment they're making to the team.

Productive Practices

The keys to good practices that are positive and goal oriented are keeping players active with numerous repetitions, using drills to improve decision making and specific skills, ensuring variety in their activities, and providing activities that are both appropriate and fun. Drills designed for small-group participation help keep kids active. Keeping kids moving reduces the possibility of discipline problems caused by boredom.

Although you should expect improvement from each player, be aware that the rate of improvement varies among individuals. Remember that players learn in different ways. Some players can be told what to do and they can do it, whereas others need a visual demonstration. I've found that introducing a skill while giving a visual demonstration and then allowing the players to try the new skill while receiving feedback from one of the coaches or from a peer is a good method of instruction. Meet with players before practice begins and explain what will happen during practice. Generally, players should review skills from previous practices and then learn a new skill. Conclude practices with player and coach assessment and feedback.

Keeping Kids' Attention

Kids love to move, and keeping their attention while instructing is sometimes difficult. Over the years I've found that certain things help. Short, concise demonstrations—limiting the amount of talking by the coach—help. Players' attention spans aren't very long, particularly those of young players, so speak clearly and concisely. Don't act as if you're on a soapbox. Goal setting helps to keep players' attention, particularly if they have had input in setting the goals. They will be more ready to listen to you if they think they suggested the goal.

I like using the huddle method when speaking to the entire group. I usually have the players sit down in a group while I remain standing so that I can make eye contact with each player. If someone is beginning to lose focus, I find another player who is doing a good job of paying attention and say something like "I really like the way Matt is being a good listener today." This positive encouragement usually influences the rest of the players to be good listeners as well. (By the way, if the sun is shining brightly, make sure the players are huddled so they aren't looking into the sun. Instead, position yourself in front of the group so that you are the one looking into the sun.)

Other tactics—such as changing the volume of your voice and your position in relation to the players—also help keep their attention. To help players on your team value being good listeners, reward them. You might say something like "You guys did such a good job listening, we're going to have 15 minutes of extra batting practice tonight." You might ask the players to develop a list of rewards they can choose from if they are good listeners. This list might include playing one of the lead-up games (see chapter 9), taking an extra drink break, or having a scrimmage-only night.

Ten Commandments of Practices

I've developed the following list to help coaches plan practices.

1. **Maintain a safe environment.** Before each practice, check the field and remove any debris. Take a rake to smooth out any rough spots in the infield caused by prior use or weather conditions. Make sure that players warming up are properly spaced and throwing in the same direction. This will help avoid players' being struck by errant tosses. Never have players warming up near or throwing toward the bench area. This will prevent players and coaches sitting on the bench from being hit with a thrown ball.

   Have designated areas where bats may be used for practice swings. Encourage players in these areas to always make a visual check of the space surrounding them before swinging the bat. Do not overlook providing the necessary equipment to prevent injury. Safety balls for the beginning players, catcher's equipment, and helmets for batters and base runners should be included in each team's equipment bag.

Make sure players drink plenty of fluids, especially during hot weather. Always carry a list of emergency phone numbers for your players, and know where the nearest phone is located. You should also have a first-aid kit, and you might want to take a first-aid course.

2. **Choose appropriate fitness activities.** Encourage all players to have a medical fitness evaluation. In some situations, doctors will offer a group rate for your organization. In most cases, however, the players' private physicians will want to examine them. Inform players and parents that any sport where there is strenuous exercise and the potential for physical contact has risks.

   Limit practices for your youngest players (ages 6 to 8) to 60 minutes or less. For older players (ages 9 and 10), practices should last between 60 and 75 minutes. For your oldest players (ages 11 to 13), practices should be limited to between 1½ and 2 hours. Remember to provide frequent water and bathroom breaks.

3. **Provide opportunities for hundreds of touches**. Use drills that allow players lots of opportunities for repetition. Encourage small-group activities to increase the opportunities for players while reducing wait time.

4. **Provide opportunities for creativity and problem solving.** Use drills that challenge players. Keep them interested and involved.

5. **Provide opportunities for skill improvement.** Use drills that allow players to learn the same skills and concepts but at different levels, if necessary. Remember to build the players' skill base progressively, making sure they are comfortable with the previous skill before moving on to more difficult ones.

   For example, when introducing fielding skills, start by explaining and demonstrating the ready position, then move on to hitting ground balls. Next, add fielding ground balls and throwing to a base, and end with fielding a ground ball and throwing to a base with base runners.

6. **Provide gamelike activities.** The more your team plays practice games, the more prepared your players will be to meet the challenges of actual game situations. Provide opportunities for your players to use the skills they have learned so far and get them to apply these skills creatively.

7. **Include small-sided games.** This is a must. Players love games, and don't enjoy wait time. Use a small-group approach to increase their

Skill Progression Chart—Fielding

Skill Progression	Activity
1) Field ground balls while stationary	1) Ready Position (drill 9)
2) Field ground balls while moving	2) Sliding (drill 16)
3) Field ground balls and throw to appropriate base	3) Infield Ground Balls (drill 33)
4) Field ground balls under gamelike conditions	4) Lead-Up Game 6

opportunities for play and keep everyone involved. Vary the small-group format by changing the number of players, the size of the space used, and the type of equipment used. Ensure that players are assigned to different groups each practice. One day, assign groups; the next day, have the players select groups. In another activity, divide the players by the color of their shirts or shoes. If you always allow kids to choose their own partners, they will tend to work only with their friends, or the best players will always want to work with each other. Players need to interact with everyone on the team. Interaction will help develop a positive environment by creating understanding and tolerance for others.

8. **Provide lots of scoring opportunities.** Players love to score runs. Provide small-sided games, games with limited fielders, and full-sided scrimmages to allow players many opportunities to score.

9. **Have fun!** It's natural to want to continue doing something you have fun with! Try to make sure your players have fun by giving them lots of gamelike activities in practices, and equal playing time during games. Above all, be sure you treat them—and they treat each other—with respect.

10. **Players should leave practice feeling good about themselves.** Everything else you do as a coach is meaningless if your players don't feel good about themselves. You can help build their self-esteem by having a sense of humor, evaluating their performance in relation to the goals you and the players have established, and developing a team relationship that is warm, respectful, and motivating. Catch them doing something good and let them know about it. Conclude each practice and game with a review of the goals the team has established. Ask players to identify someone on the team they thought did a great job toward meeting the team goals. This helps build a sense of community within the team.

Time Management

The best way I've found to manage practice time efficiently is to have a written outline for each practice (see Practice Session Worksheet next page). Include a list of activities and drills in the order they will be practiced, the amount of time allocated to each activity, and any other notes you may have. You may want to post this information on the backstop so players can check before practice to see what the first activity will be, what the batting practice order will be, and so forth.

Allocation of time and activities will vary according to the goals of each practice. Take time to assess your practice plan by asking these questions.

- Does my plan have clear purposes and objectives?
- Is my plan reasonable?
- Is my plan relevant?
- Is my plan workable?

If the answers to these questions are all "yes," then you probably have a good plan. Remember to make sure your plan is age- and skill-appropriate.

Backstops with side extensions help keep players and coaches safe during games.

Practice Session Worksheet
(for 9- and 10-year-olds)

Team meeting (5 min.): Discuss the week's schedule and explain today's practice.

Warm-up (stretching, throwing, and catching) (15 min.):

Stretch individually
Throw and catch with partner
Drill 5: Short-Short-Long Throwing

Station work (divide players into three groups of four to six players; every 10 minutes, the groups rotate to the next station—players at station 3 go to station 1):

Station 1: Batting (10 min.): Live batting practice in infield

Station 2: Fielding (10 min.): Drill 18: Rolling Cone (in outfield)

Station 3: Baserunning (10 min.): Drill 109: Go/Back Base Running (in outfield)

Break (5 min.)

Scrimmage game (20 min.): Full-team scrimmage

Cool-down/review (10 min.):

Review practice and collect fund-raiser money

Troubleshooting Chart

Use this chart as a quick way to find brief analyses of and suggested solutions for some of the common problems of young baseball players.

Problem	Analysis	Solution
Players don't throw accurately.	May be caused by a lack of balance and arm speed, the pathway of the hand during the throwing motion, or failure to finish the throw by pointing at the target.	Provide lots of opportunities for throwing and catching skills in partner and small-group work, stressing good mechanics as in drills 1–3. Combine throwing accuracy with decision making as in drills 4–7, 33, and 76–78.
Players aren't ready to field the ball when it is hit to them.	Young players become distracted easily. Sometimes players aren't taught how to position themselves to be ready for the ball.	Reinforce the concept of being ready before the ball is hit as in drills 9, 34, 35, 44, and 70–73.
Positioning of the glove for fielding and catching is difficult for some players.	Cause may be as simple as a player using a glove that is too big and heavy, or more complicated, such as not understanding how to rotate the thumb of the glove inward when crossing the midline of the body and raising the glove above the waist. Players' ability to track the ball with their eyes could also affect glove positioning.	Players need to have a glove that fits appropriately. They also need to be taught how to change the position of the glove correctly as in drills 10 and 11. Tracking skills and crossing the midline for players struggling with these concepts can be developed by using drill 12.
Collisions sometimes occur with two or more players trying to field a ball.	Collisions occur because players don't understand personal space concepts and/or they lack communication or vision skills.	Provide practice opportunities to develop understanding of personal space concepts as in drills 13 and 14 and communication skills as in drills 28–30 and 74, 75, and 80.
Players have a difficult time fielding balls that aren't hit directly at them.	Fielders may not begin in a ready position, may lack the ability to move laterally efficiently, or may not understand the best method of getting to the ball.	Teach players the fundamental movements required to move to the ball. These include the slide step as in drills 15–18; the crossover step as in drills 19, 20, and 22; and charging the ball as in drills 24 and 25.
Players misplay routine ground balls consistently.	Players may lack eye-hand coordination and/or reflexes to make subtle adjustments when fielding. Fielding techniques may suffer due to lack of experience.	Development of these skills takes lots of repetitions. Provide hundreds of opportunities to improve eye-hand coordination and reflexes during such small-group partner drills as drills 21, 22, and 26. If necessary, review glove positioning. Struggling players should begin by fielding ground balls from a stationary position and then advance to moving while fielding.

(continued next page)

Troubleshooting Chart (continued)

Problem	Analysis	Solution
Fly balls aren't being caught consistently.	Tracking skills, being in a ready position, movement to the ball, and communication between teammates all affect catching fly balls efficiently.	Small-group activities with lots of repetitions will help develop the skills necessary for catching fly balls. Begin with a drill like 27, which has players catching fly balls while stationary. As the players progress, add drills for movement and communication as in drills 28–31, 79, and 80. For variety, use a tennis ball and tennis racket to hit the fly balls.
Players are timid when at bat for fear of getting struck with the ball.	Players lack confidence in their ability and/or technique in avoiding being hit by a pitched ball. They realize the ball is hard and will hurt them if they're hit.	First build confidence by teaching the turn away technique as in drills 81 and 82. To help avoid injuries, use fleece balls until the technique is mastered. Also help players understand the proper position for hitting in relationship to the distance from the plate as in drill 83.
Players throw the bat when they swing.	Cause may be associated with a poor grip and/or releasing the grip during the swing. Other contributors may be the force of the swing and the size of the bat.	Teach players the proper grip as in drill 84. Use drill 85 to insist that players finish the swing by placing the bat on a game spot. Encourage players to use a bat that is an appropriate size and weight.
Players make poor contact when hitting.	Cause may be the lack of development of eye-hand coordination, taking a large stride, stepping away from the plate with the front foot (bailing out), stepping forward with the back foot, having an inefficient swing pattern, or not understanding the strike zone.	Use small-group activities through station work to teach the elements of hitting. Drills 86–88, 93, 97, and 99 will help develop eye-hand coordination. Drills 89–91 will help reinforce how to stride properly. Drill 92 will help players eliminate stepping forward with the back foot, while drills 94, 96, and 98 will help develop an efficient swing pattern. Drill 95 will help give players a better understanding of the strike zone.
Bunting the ball is a real problem for our team.	Poor bunting can result from not understanding proper bunting technique for the various types of bunts used. Bunting balls out of the strike zone, unless a suicide squeeze, will also produce poor bunting results.	Teach players proper techniques for bunting in situations that include sacrifice bunts, bunting for a base hit, and squeeze bunts using drills 100–105.
Our team seldom has a big inning because of baserunning mistakes.	Poor baserunning can be the result of a lack of communication between coaches and players or poor judgment by players and/or coaches. It may also result from poor baserunning technique.	Include in practice sessions small-group and whole-group activities that emphasize good baserunning technique as in drills 108–115. Lots of repetition and the development of good communication between players and coaches will produce better baserunning results.

Questions and Answers

Coaches often ask me for advice on how to solve problems they're having with their teams. Although the names and locations differ, the problems are similar.

Q. I have a team of 9- and 10-year-olds. Our games take forever to play because they consist mostly of walking and stealing. How can we improve this situation?

A. I had a similar experience the first year I coached youth baseball. We organized a meeting for coaches and league officials to discuss what we wanted for the kids as opposed to what was actually happening. As a result, we instituted a no-walk, no-steal rule. If a pitcher walked a batter, a batting tee was placed at home plate and the batter was allowed to hit the ball off the tee. This decision allowed batters to strike the ball and fielders to get lots of opportunities for fielding the ball and making decisions, while the length of the game was reduced because there were more outs being made by the fielders. The no-steal rule enabled fielders to have more force-outs during play.

Q. I coach a baseball team of 9- and 10-year-olds. Some of my players want to play positions they aren't skilled enough to play. What should I do?

A. Many factors contribute to the development of a skilled player. Remember that children develop at different rates. It is difficult to determine what kind of player a 9-year-old will be in five or six years. I would let players experience many different positions. They may not be highly skilled as yet, but with lots of repetition, positive feedback, and encouragement, they will have their best chance for success. An exception to this suggestion would be if you felt that playing someone in a particular position would jeopardize that player's safety.

Q. I have players who pitch well on the sideline, but when they get in the game they can't seem to throw a strike. How can I help them?

A. Try to make warming up as gamelike as possible. It the players are pitching off a mound during the game, it may be possible to construct mounds on the sidelines for warm-ups. Also, after the pitchers warm up for a few minutes, have a hitter stand next to the plate without swinging to simulate an actual game. Make sure the hitter takes some pitches on both sides of the plate. Finally, have your pitchers warm up by throwing in the same direction they would in the game. This will allow them to adjust to the sun and wind.

Q. I have 16 players on my team. How can I keep them all busy?

A. In my years of coaching, I have seen many practice situations where the coach is pitching, one player is hitting, and the rest of the team is mostly standing around. It doesn't have to be this way. Kids love being active, and their skills will have a better chance to develop if they get lots of repetitions through a practice framework that provides multiple station work. Divide the players into groups of three to five players, and set up three or four stations to engage them in skill development. Use assistant coaches to help players keep focus and to maintain a safe environment.

Q. We have batting practice twice a week. During games, we just don't seem to be making good contact. How can we improve our batting?

A. Try running batting practice by using station work to increase the amount of repetitions each player receives. Set up one station in a safe space in the outfield where players are using a batting tee. Have an assistant coach at the station observe and give feedback, including visual demonstration, to correct flaws. Set up a whiffle ball station in the opposite side of the outfield. Let players pitch using whiffle balls so that players experience hitting a ball pitched by someone their own size. An assistant can stand near the hitter to observe and correct.

At a third station behind the backstop, have a coach toss canvas-covered safety balls to a batter, who strikes the ball into the fence. As the coach is tossing, he or she should also observe and make corrections where appropriate. At a fourth station, have another coach conduct a live batting practice. Have the players rotate through a station every 15 minutes. It will take an hour to complete the rotations, but the result will be lots of repetitions and numerous opportunities for teaching. Of course, a batting practice of this nature requires the help of assistant coaches. Recruiting volunteers to fill these positions should be a top priority.

Q. One of my players doesn't come to practice but wants to play in the games. How do I handle this situation?

A. First, discuss practice attendance at your preseason meeting. Explain that players need to practice skills to improve the quality of their play, so practice time should be valued. If the situation persists, communication with parents is the best way to handle it. If a player misses practice, talk to a parent and find out why. There may have been another family commitment or an emergency, or maybe a parent had to work overtime and a ride was not available. Make parents aware at the preseason meeting that alternatives, including car pools, are available if transportation is a problem.

Since most of your players are not responsible for their own transportation, it is difficult to hold players accountable for what they can't control. That's why a rule like "If you don't practice, you don't play in the game" may be inappropriate at the youth level. Whatever you decide, be consistent. If you decide to have a no-practice, no-play rule, enforce it consistently. If you decide to treat each case individually, show the same understanding and flexibility for each player.

Q. I have 15 boys and 1 girl on my team. How should I handle this situation?

A. In my first year of coaching youth baseball, I had a similar situation. Think of your team not as 15 boys and 1 girl but instead as 16 players who love the game of baseball and want to improve their quality of play. Love of sport and striving for improvement have no gender bias. Build a culture of respect for all players by recognizing individual strengths and pointing out the need for improvement in areas of weakness.

Q. None of the parents of players on my team has volunteered to help. What can I do?

A. Sometimes parents are willing to help but won't volunteer without being asked. At your preseason meeting, let parents know how much more successful their children's season will be with the addition of assistant coaches to implement practice plans that include multiple stations. Clearly define the volunteers' roles, and have a sign-up sheet at the meeting. If you still receive no responses, consider other options. Older brothers or sisters or other relatives may be interested. Advertise in the community for help. Lots of adults who aren't parents are interested in baseball and in helping kids. Ask the local high school baseball coach for the names of players who might be interested in working with a youth baseball team.

CHAPTER 3

Throwing Drills

Throwing is a fundamental baseball skill. Throwing accuracy and speed can be developed through partner and small-group activities. Beginning players should be given hundreds of opportunities to develop throwing skills at practices while they are introduced to correct throwing technique involving both upper- and lower-body mechanics.

Upper-body mechanics for the overhand throw involve moving the throwing hand from in front of the body past the ear located on the same side as the throwing hand. At the same time, the shoulders rotate in a coiling motion. As the shoulders uncoil, the arm is thrust forward. The ball is released with the throwing hand pointing toward the target. The hips rotate with the shoulders during this coiling action. The legs on the dominant side (throwing side) generate force by flexing during the coiling action and extending during the uncoiling process. The foot on the dominant side pivots according to the amount of coiling, then is used to push off with to help generate the force for the throw. The nondominant foot (the left foot for right-handed throws) moves in a forward motion toward the target. This action helps to balance the lower body during the throw. Many younger players need to be constantly reminded to step with the opposite foot to maintain their balance.

Emphasize the throw's coiling action more with intermediate and advanced players, for whom throwing velocity becomes more of a factor. Footwork for intermediate and advanced players when fielding, including the crow-hop, is discussed in chapter 4.

When practicing throwing skills, use good safety techniques. If engaged in partner work, have groups of partners throwing in the same direction and spaced so that injuring another player with an errant throw is impossible. To reduce the possibility of injury, never have players practice throwing skills near the bench or areas where spectators are gathered. Modify equipment to meet the needs of the players. Beginning players should use some kind of safety ball that has the approximate weight and size of a regular baseball.

Players by position			
1	pitcher	H	home plate
2	catcher	1	1st base
3	1st base	2	2nd base
4	2nd base	3	3rd base
5	3rd base	- - - ->	thrown ball
6	shortstop	——→	run
7	left fielder	(symbol)	rolled ball
8	center fielder	(symbol)	underhand toss
9	right fielder	C	coach
		(symbol)	game marker
		(symbol)	game spot

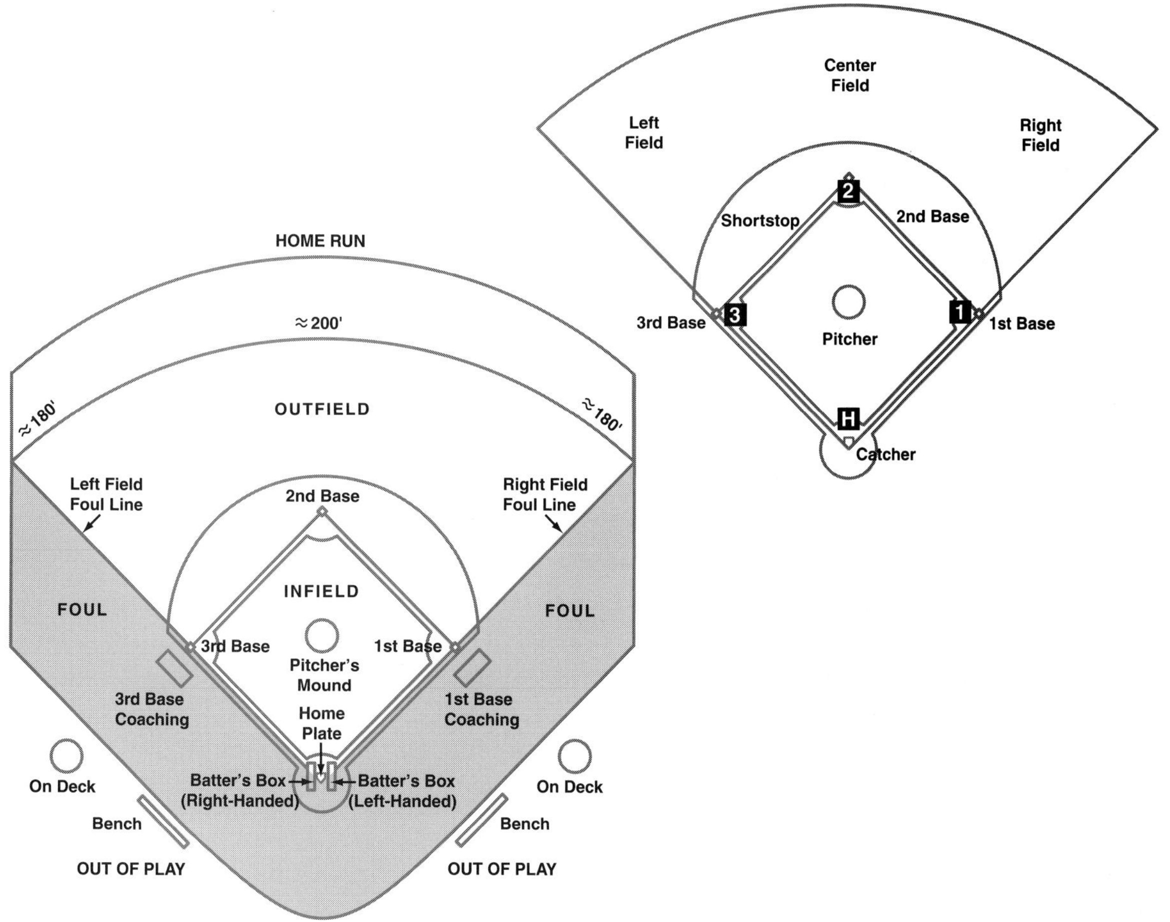

1. Partner Throwing

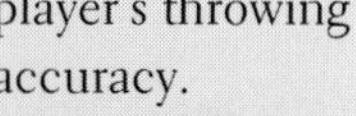

Purpose:
To develop the player's throwing accuracy.
Number of Players:
2
Equipment:
1 safety ball,
2 game markers
Time:
5 to 7 minutes

1. Position two game markers 5 feet apart.
2. The players stand on opposite sides of an imaginary line between the markers.
3. One of the players throws the ball to the other player.
4. Each time a player completes a throw to her partner, she takes one step backward.
5. Players count how many throws they can make before they make an errant throw; the ball shouldn't touch the ground.

This is a throwing drill, so players who drop the ball aren't penalized. Encourage players to step forward with the nondominant foot (the foot opposite the player's throwing side) as they push off the dominant foot. The throwing, or dominant, hand moves backward past the ear on the dominant side, then quickly thrusts forward, and should point toward the target at the throw's completion. To get the speed needed to throw longer distances, players need to accelerate the forward movement of the throwing hand. Beginning players should use safety balls to reduce injuries caused by deficient catching skills.

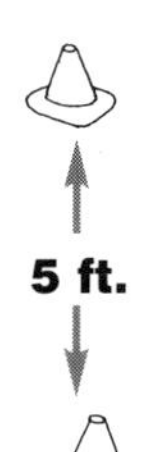

2. One-Knee Throwing

Purpose:
To improve the player's upper-body throwing mechanics.
Number of Players:
2
Equipment:
1 safety ball
Time:
5 to 10 minutes

1. Position players 15 feet apart.
2. Players kneel on the dominant-side knee.
3. The player with the ball throws to his partner.
4. Players repeat this until the time is up.

This simple drill is sometimes necessary for beginning players struggling with the mechanics of the overhand throw. Kneeling eliminates the lower-body action and allows the players and coaches to concentrate on the upper-body movement. Encourage players to move their throwing hand in a backward motion past the ear on the dominant side. As part of this movement, the shoulder of the throwing arm rotates away from the target, then begins a forward motion, which initiates the forward movement of the throwing arm and hand. Remind players to finish the throw with the hand pointed toward the target.

15 ft.

3. Standing with Nondominant Foot in Front

Purpose: To reinforce stepping with the opposite foot during the throwing motion.

Number of Players: 3
Equipment: 1 safety ball
Time: 10 to 12 minutes

1. Position players in a line.
2. A coach stands 10 feet in front of the players.
3. The first player places her nondominant foot in front of her dominant foot.
4. Stepping forward slightly with the nondominant foot, the player throws to the coach.
5. Repeat with each player several times.
6. After players have executed this movement properly, they change to begin with their feet together, then step forward with the nondominant foot.
7. Repeat.

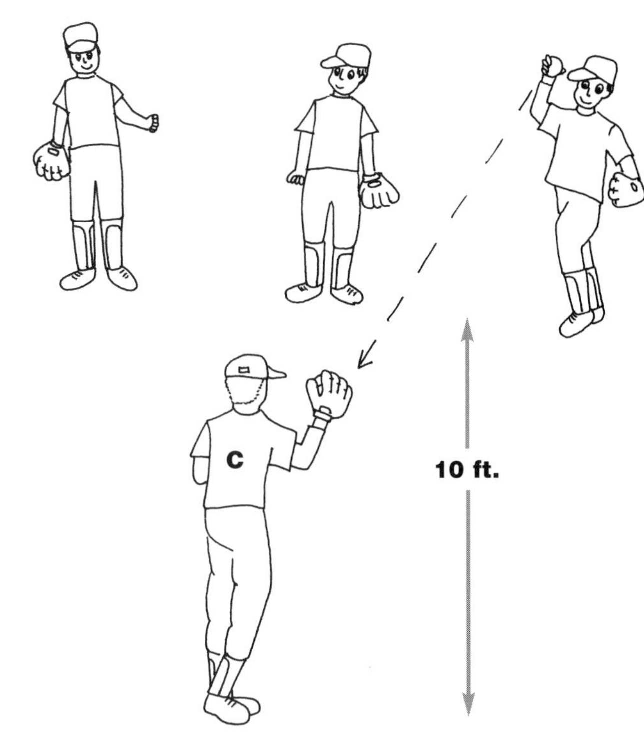

The correct throwing motion is executed by stepping forward with the nondominant foot—that is, the foot opposite the throwing arm. Beginning players sometimes step forward with the dominant foot. Correct this tendency early, before it becomes a pattern. Starting the throwing motion with the nondominant foot already forward helps players get the feel of the correct motion. The correct throwing motion allows players to keep their balance and to generate more arm speed by shifting the body weight from the dominant foot to the nondominant foot while rotating the hips and shoulders.

Proper throwing position.

4. Two-Team Throwing

Purpose: To develop the player's throwing accuracy and speed.

Number of Players: 8
Equipment: 2 baseballs
Time: 12 to 15 minutes

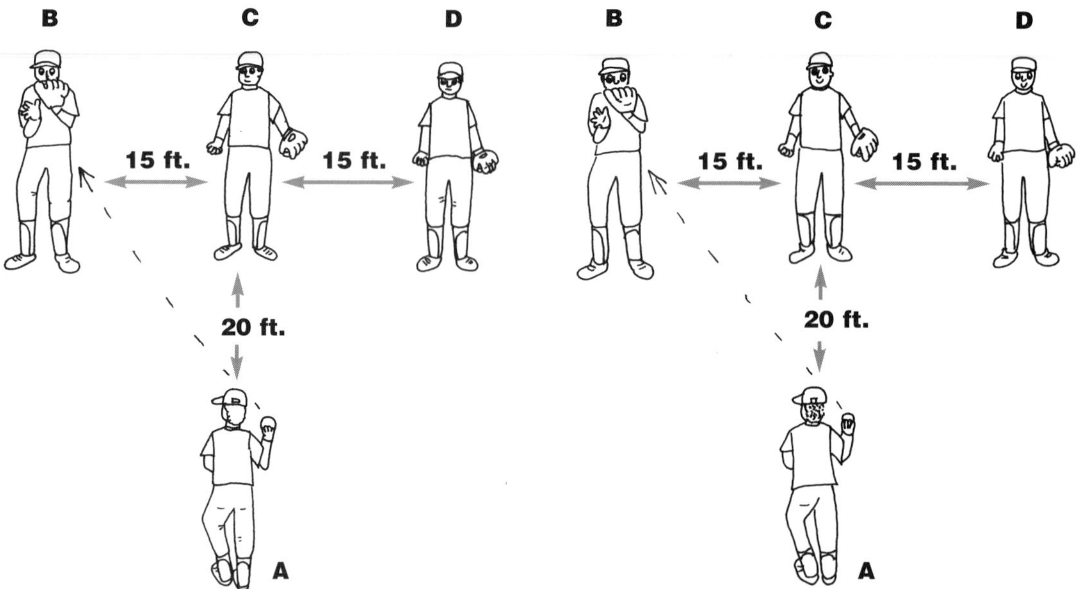

1. Divide players into two teams of four players.
2. Position three players 15 feet apart in a straight line.
3. Position a fourth player 20 feet in front of the line of players.
4. On the coach's signal, player A from each team throws the ball to player B. Player B returns it to player A.
5. Player A repeats the throw to players C and D, both of whom return the toss to player A.
6. This action continues; each time a player catches the ball counts as 1 point.
7. The first team to reach 21 points wins.

Players need opportunities to practice catching, stepping, and throwing quickly because these situations frequently occur in game situations. Encourage players to use overhand throws to prevent the ball from curving, which sometimes occurs with sidearm throws.

5. Short-Short-Long Throwing

Purpose: To develop the player's concept that throwing various distances requires different arm action.

Number of Players: 3
Equipment: 1 baseball
Time: 5 to 7 minutes

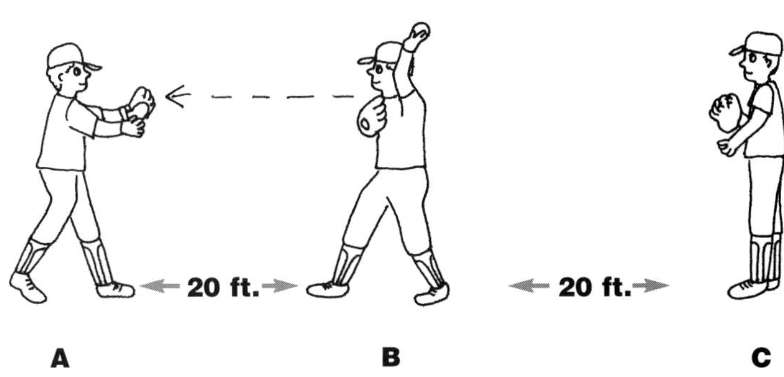

1. Position players in a line so that player B is 20 feet from player A and player C is 20 feet from player B and 40 feet from player A.
2. Player B throws to player A, then runs toward player A's position.
3. Player A throws to player C.
4. Player A runs to assume a position 20 feet from player C previously vacated by player B.
5. Player C throws to player A.
6. Player A throws back to player C, then runs toward player C's position.
7. Player C throws to player B, then runs to assume the middle position just vacated by player A.
8. Player B then throws to player A.
9. Repeat.

Throwing the ball at different distances requires different arm action. Arm speed is slower for shorter distances than for longer distances. Although the throwing mechanics are the same, the hip and shoulder rotation is faster for longer throws, allowing the arm and hand to generate more speed. The faster the hand moves forward from behind the ear, the more velocity the ball has.

6. Triangle Throwing 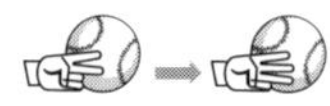

Purpose: To develop the player's catch-pivot-throw technique.

Number of Players: 3
Equipment: 1 baseball, 3 game markers
Time: 5 to 7 minutes

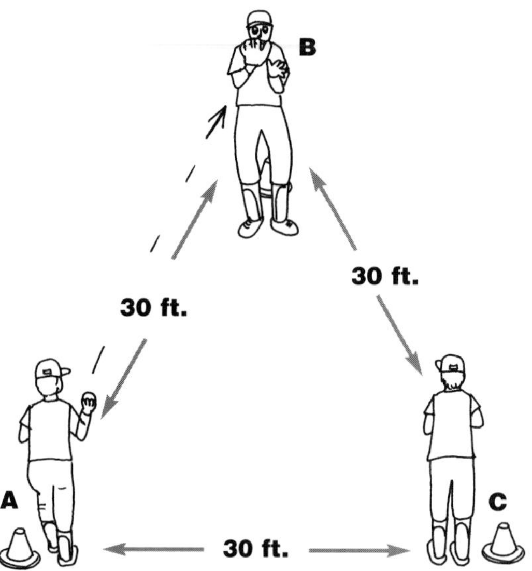

1. Position players in a triangle designated by game markers 30 feet apart.
2. Player A throws to player B.
3. Player B catches the ball, executes a jump-pivot, and throws the ball to player C.
4. Player C catches the ball, does a jump-pivot, and throws to player A.
5. Players repeat.

For players to throw accurately, they must square themselves up to their target. The jump-pivot is executed by jumping and simultaneously turning in the air with both feet in the direction of the target. This action allows players to throw with more velocity and accuracy because they're facing their target. An alternative to the jump-pivot is for players to catch the ball and turn their feet to a throwing position without jumping. This action would be too slow in play, but beginning players might feel more comfortable doing it once or twice to help them get the idea of the drill before graduating to the jump-pivot.

7. Star Throwing

Purpose: To develop the player's throwing accuracy.

Number of Players: 5
Equipment: 1 baseball
Time: 5 to 7 minutes

1. Position players 30 feet from each other in the shape of a star.
2. Player A throws the ball to player C.
3. Player C throws the ball to the player who didn't throw to him and who is not standing to his right or left. This would be player E.
4. The action continues with the player who catches the ball throwing to the player who didn't throw to him and who is not to his right or left.

This drill combines throwing skills with decision making. Encourage players to step, catch, and throw. The throw should be delivered overhand with the throwing hand pointed at the target on release.

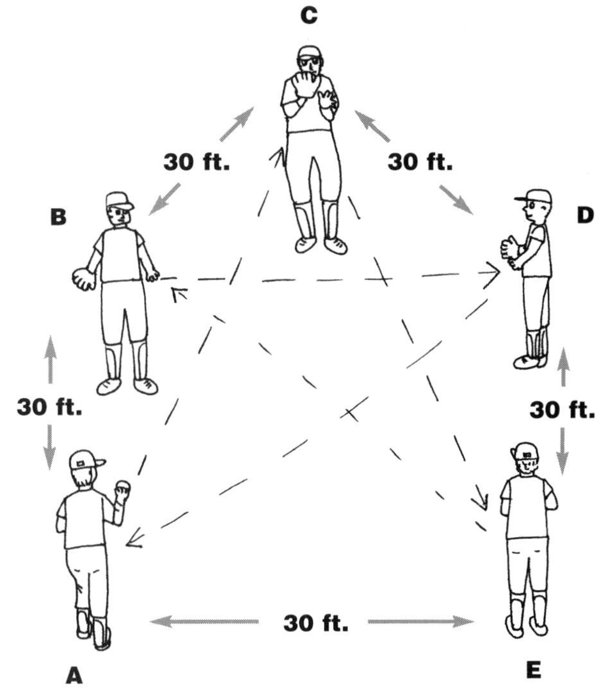

CHAPTER 4

Fielding Drills

Fielding is another fundamental skill of baseball. Good fielding skills are acquired through modeling and repetition. Players should have hundreds of chances for developing fielding skills at each practice. Using small-group activities through station work provides lots of action for players. Plan your practices to use the small-group activities in this chapter with a group of players while other players are engaged in batting practice or other stations. Use assistant coaches to demonstrate skills, observe and correct techniques, and supervise activities at these stations. This helps ensure continuous action and promote a positive attitude in players.

This chapter includes activities to develop skills for fielding both ground balls and balls in the air. The drills focus on fielding techniques, including various ready positions for infielders and outfielders and glove positions for balls above and below the waist and to the left and right of midline. Various ways of moving to the ball, such as the slide step, the crossover step, and charging the slowly hit ball, are also discussed. This chapter also includes the crow-hop, a footwork technique executed when throwing after fielding a ball. This step-together-step action allows players to transition smoothly from a fielding position to a throwing position.

Fielding technique is only part of the fielding process. Players—particularly beginners—need to understand that although fielding skills may be individual, they are part of a team's effort to produce outs. For example, beginning players must realize that the fastest way to get a player out who has hit a ground ball to an infielder other than the first-base player is to throw the ball to the base. Many beginning players will try to run the ball to the base themselves. To avoid unnecessary collisions, beginning players also need to understand and respect other players' spaces. Of course, intermediate and advanced players also need reinforcement in this concept. Use the small-group activities in this chapter that are designed to move players in relationship to one another and to teach player communication.

As always, modify equipment to meet players' needs. Use safety balls, sponge balls, rubber balls, and so forth when teaching beginning players new techniques, particularly when these techniques involve crossing the midline of the body. Such additional equipment as tennis rackets and tennis balls to strike balls in the air can add a change of pace, even for advanced players, and can be very motivating. Encourage parents to provide the players with gloves that are of appropriate size and weight.

8. Getting an Out 

Purpose: To develop the concept that it's faster to throw a ball to a base to get a runner out than it is to run the ball to the base.

Number of Players: 3
Equipment: 1 safety ball
Time: 8 to 10 minutes

Note key to symbols, page 21

1. Position a fielder at the pitcher's mound and another at first base.
2. Instruct the third player to be a base runner starting from home plate.
3. Standing at home plate, a coach rolls the ball to the player at the pitcher's mound. As soon as the coach rolls the ball, the base runner begins running to first base.
4. The coach instructs the fielder to pick up the rolled ball and run it to first base to get the runner out.
5. The action is repeated, but this time the coach instructs the fielder to pick up the ball and throw it to first base.

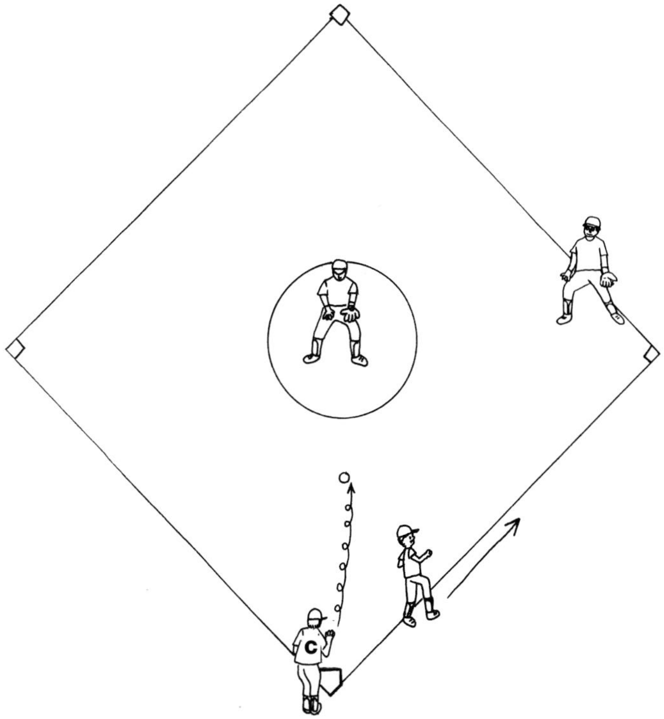

Do this drill first with the whole team watching. Beginning players must understand that throwing the ball is a faster way to get the ball to a base than running it there. After instructing the whole group, break the group down into smaller parts so that all of the players have a chance to participate in the activity.

9. Ready Position

Purpose: To develop the concept of the ready position for fielding.

Number of Players: 3
Equipment: 1 safety ball
Time: 5 to 7 minutes

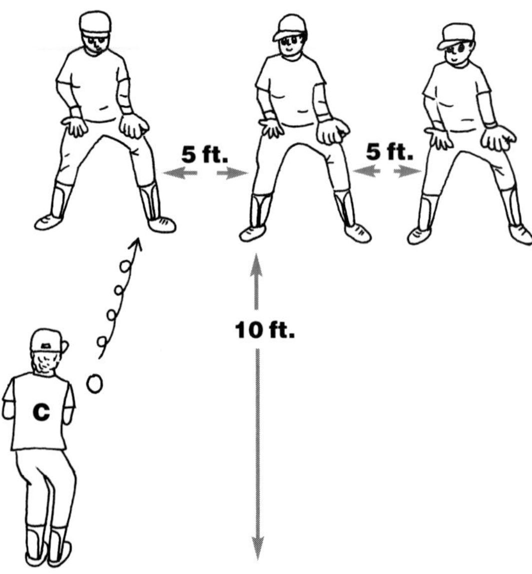

1. Position players in a line 5 feet apart from each other.
2. Standing 10 feet in front of the line, a coach says "ready position."
3. The players assume a ready position stance.
4. The coach rolls the ball to one of the players.
5. The player fielding the ball throws it back to the coach.
6. Repeat with each player in the line.

Some infielders like to set their bodies in motion by slowly taking a few small steps toward the hitter. For beginning and intermediate players without previous experience, however, the ready position should involve the knees and waist being flexed, weight slightly forward on the balls of the feet, head up watching the direction of the ball, feet shoulder width apart, with the glove opened and down near the ground. As players sees the direction and speed of the ball, they move accordingly, moving right, left, and forward for slower balls. Have beginning players watch the ball until it is in their glove. This will ensure they keep their head down, improving their ability to track the ball. Encourage players to keep the ball in front of them when fielding, if possible, instead of playing balls to their side. This will allow them to knock down a ball that takes a bad hop, and they will still be able to make the play.

10. Glove Positioning

Purpose: To develop the technique of changing the position of the glove to catch balls above and below the waist.

Number of Players: 3
Equipment: 1 safety ball
Time: 8 to 10 minutes

1. Position players in a line 5 feet apart from each other.
2. A coach stands 6 feet in front of the line.
3. The coach tosses a ball below the waist of the first player.
4. Repeat for each player several times.
5. The coach begins with the first player again by tossing the ball above the player's waist.
6. Repeat for each player several times.
7. The coach then tosses to any player, above or below the waist, in no particular order.

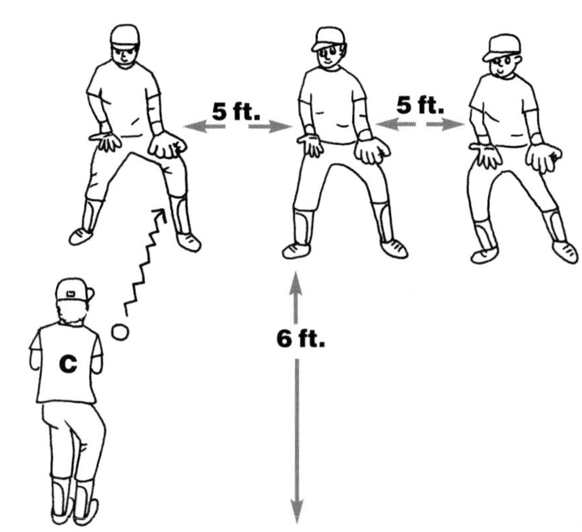

Small-group work allows players many chances to refine their skills. Before beginning this drill, give players a visual demonstration of how to assume a ready position: legs flexed, torso bent at waist, feet shoulder width apart, glove opened below knees with palms facing up. Then demonstrate how to move the glove by rotating the thumb inward and facing the palm away to catch balls that are thrown above the waist. Performing lots of repetition in drills like this one improves skills and reduces injuries.

11. Crossing Midline

Purpose: To develop the technique of crossing the midline of the body to catch the ball.

Number of Players: 3
Equipment: 1 safety ball
Time: 8 to 10 minutes

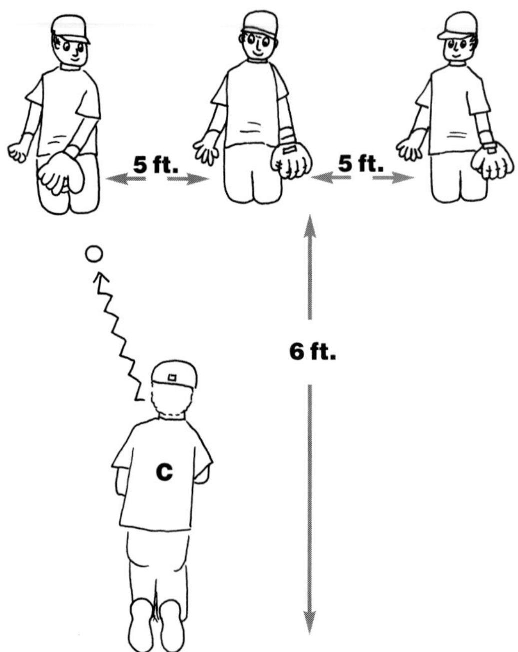

1. Position players on their knees in a line 5 feet apart from each other.
2. A coach kneels 6 feet in front of the line.
3. The coach tosses the ball to the glove side of the first player. The player catches the ball and returns it to the coach.
4. Repeat for all players.
5. The coach tosses the ball to the throwing side of each player.
6. The coach tosses the ball several times to each player, alternating between tossing the ball above and below the player's waist.
7. The coach tosses the ball to the right or left of each player. The player has to decide which way to maneuver the glove to make the catch.

Having players kneel reduces movement of the lower body and allows players to concentrate on movement of their glove. Before beginning this drill, demonstrate how to cross the midline of the body with the glove hand. Do this without the glove on so players can visualize how the thumb of the nondominant hand rotates downward with the palm facing away from the player. This rotation is greater when catching balls below the waist. Beginning players will often cross the midline of the body with the glove while keeping their palm facing upward. This not only is awkward but can cause injury if the ball bounces off the heel of the glove and strikes them.

12. Scarf Midline 

Purpose: To develop the technique of crossing the midline of the body with the glove hand.

Number of Players: 1
Equipment: 1 scarf
Time: 5 to 7 minutes

1. Position the player 5 feet from a coach.
2. The coach tosses a scarf to the player's throwing side.
3. The player must cross the midline of his body and catch the scarf with his glove hand.
4. The player returns the scarf to the coach, and the action is repeated.
5. The coach varies the throws above and below the player's waist.

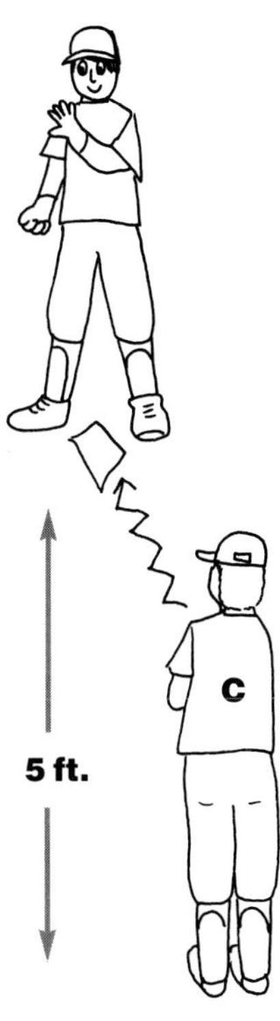

Players' skills develop at different rates. For beginning players struggling with the concept of crossing the midline of the body, the scarf drill provides them lots of repetition with the movement while offering a nonthreatening way for players to develop the reflexes and turning associated with this movement. Players can practice this movement at home by tossing a scarf to themselves across the body and catching it. The scarf allows more reaction time for players to be successful until their skill improves enough to use safety balls.

13. Personal Space 

Purpose: To develop the concept of personal space for fielding.

Number of Players: 2
Equipment: 1 safety ball, 4 game markers
Time: 5 to 7 minutes

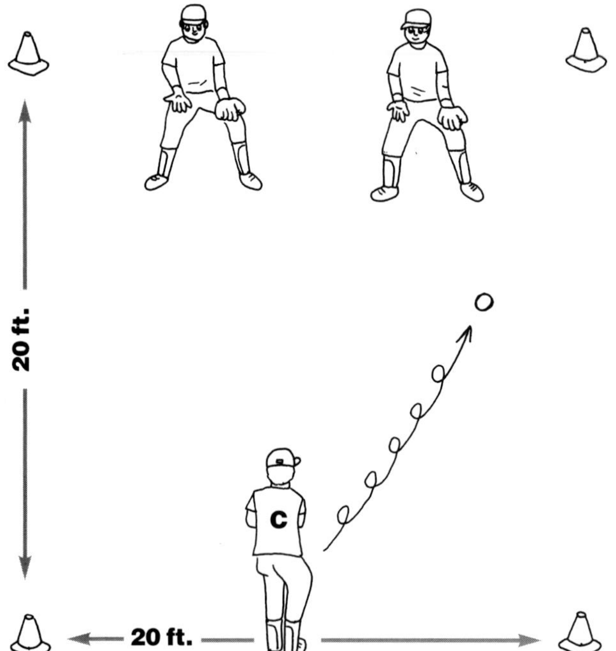

1. Use four game markers to make a 20-by-20-foot grid.
2. Position players in one end of the grid, one on each side.
3. A coach rolls a safety ball to one side of the grid.
4. The player on that side fields the ball and throws it back to the coach.
5. The coach continues by rolling the ball to the left, the right, and the middle.
6. The appropriate player fields the ball and throws it back to the coach. For a ball in the middle, players must communicate to decide who will field the ball.

Beginning players see the ball and react to it without respecting another player's territory (personal space). You will often see a ball hit in a T-ball game and several players swarming over it. Drills designed to teach spacing concepts help prevent swarming and reduce the possibility of injury. Instruct players in this drill that when the ball is moving in another player's territory, they should let that player field it. When the ball is in the middle, players must communicate with each other to determine who will field the ball.

14. Spacing Game

Purpose: To develop spacing concepts when fielding.

Number of Players: 3
Equipment: 5 safety balls, 1 bat, 4 game markers
Time: 8 to 10 minutes

1. Use four game markers to make a 30-by-30-foot grid.
2. Position players in one end of the grid.
3. A coach stands at the other end of the grid and attempts to hit a ground ball that will roll past the players at the opposite end of the grid.
4. The coach hits five balls, earning 1 point for each ball hit past the opposite side of the grid.
5. Fielders receive 1 point for each ball they stop from going past the opposite end.
6. The fielder with the most points in five attempts wins.

Instruct the players to space themselves properly because standing together won't allow them to cover adequately all of the space in which the ball may be hit. To give a group of players a greater challenge, increase the size of the grid accordingly.

15. Slide Step

Purpose: To develop the slide step for fielding ground balls.

Number of Players: 2
Equipment: 1 safety ball or baseball
Time: 5 to 7 minutes

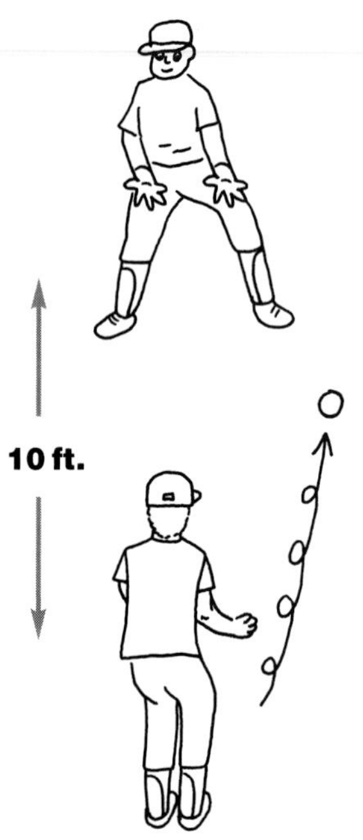

1. Position players 10 feet apart without gloves. One player has a ball.
2. The player with the ball rolls it to his partner's left side.
3. The player fielding the ball executes the slide step, picks up the ball, and uses an underhand toss to return it to his partner.
4. The player fielding the ball then slides back to his starting position, and his partner rolls the ball to the right fielder's side. The fielder executes the slide step to the right and fields the ball.
5. The fielding player has 10 opportunities, 5 right and 5 left, to execute the slide step.
6. After 10 rolls, the players reverse roles.
7. Repeat.

The slide step is used when a player can move to a ground ball that is not hit too far to his right or left. The player moves the foot closest to the direction of the ball sideways and slides the other foot toward it. If more than one slide step is necessary, the steps should be executed quickly to place the player in position to field the ball before it arrives. This drill also reinforces the concept of staying down, bending at the waist, and watching the ball into the hands when fielding. For beginning players, use a safety ball. Use a regular baseball for intermediate and advanced players.

16. Sliding

Purpose: To develop technique for fielding ground balls when in motion.

Number of Players: 3
Equipment: 2 safety balls or baseballs, 4 game markers
Time: 8 to 10 minutes

1. Use four game markers to make a 20-by-20-foot grid.
2. Position two players in one end of the grid, each with a glove and a ball.
3. Position the third player with a glove in one corner of the opposite end of the grid.
4. Player B rolls a ball toward the empty corner on player C's end.
5. Player C fields the ball and throws it back to player B.
6. Player A rolls a ball to the corner player C vacated.
7. Player C moves back to the corner in which she started, fields the ball, and throws it back to player A.
8. Continue these back-and-forth movements.
9. After 1 minute, change positions.

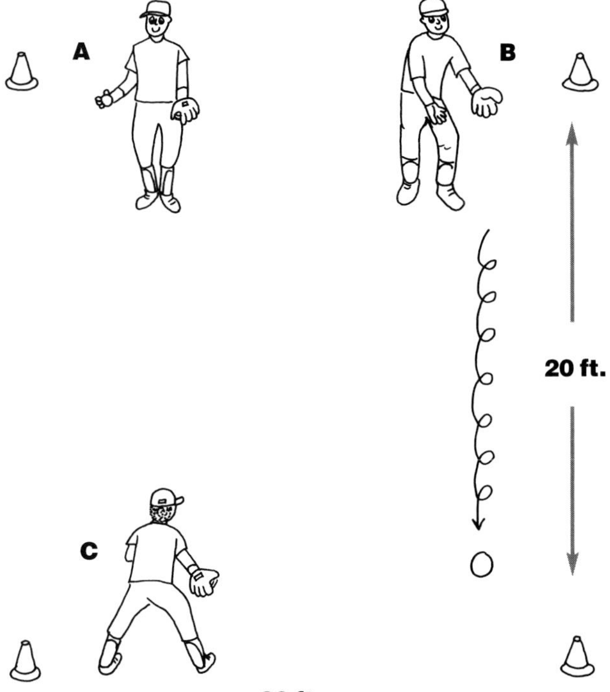

Beginning players need to understand that they must go to the space where the ball is traveling if they want to field it. Standing still provides little coverage. Movement is the key. This drill will get players moving. It is fast-paced, so beginners and intermediate players change roles every minute. Use safety balls for beginner players and baseballs for intermediate players.

17. Return to Sender 

Purpose: To develop the slide step for fielding ground balls.

Number of Players: 10
Equipment: 5 safety balls or baseballs, 4 game markers
Time: 5 to 7 minutes

1. Use four game markers to make a 30-by-30-foot grid.
2. Divide the players into five teams of two.
3. Position the teams in the grid. One partner in each team has a ball and will remain stationary.
4. The partner with the ball rolls it to the left or right of her partner.
5. The partner without the ball uses a slide step to field the ball, tosses it back to her partner, and then moves to find another partner who is holding a ball in a stationary position.
6. Continue the action for 30 seconds, then switch roles between players who were moving and those who were stationary.

Executing the slide step efficiently helps players successfully move to balls hit to their right or left. Encourage players to move to the ball quickly while keeping their legs and hips flexed. Use safety balls for beginning players and baseballs for intermediate players.

18. Rolling Cone

Purpose: To develop the slide step for fielding ground balls.

Number of Players: 5
Equipment: 1 safety ball or baseball, 8 game markers
Time: 8 to 10 minutes

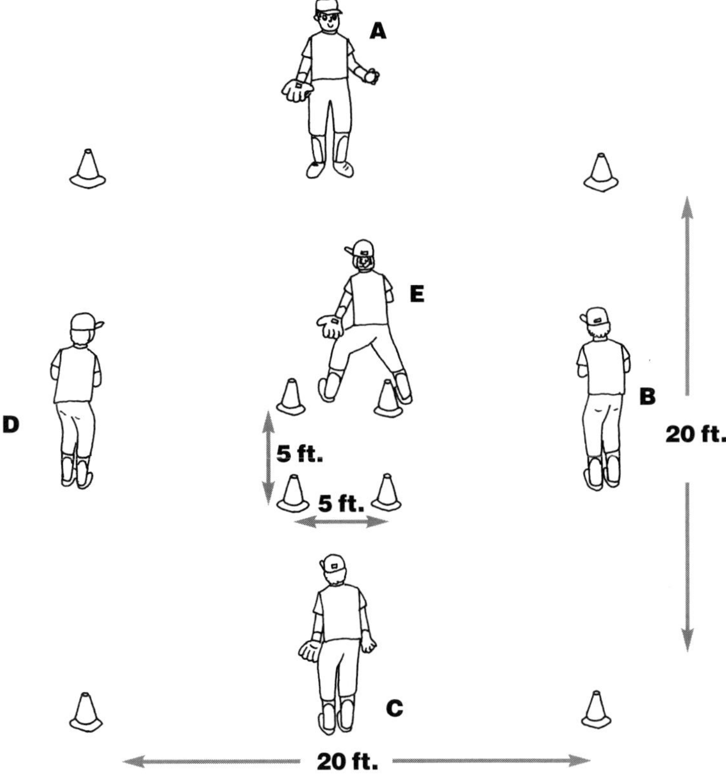

1. Use four game markers to make a 20-by-20-foot grid. Use an additional four game markers to make a 5-by-5-foot grid within the larger grid.
2. Position one player on each side of the larger grid. Position a fifth player (player E) outside the smaller grid.
3. Instruct players on the sides of the larger grid to roll the ball between two of the markers of the smaller grid. Player E tries to prevent this by fielding any balls that are rolled toward the grid.
4. Player A has possession of the ball first. He may choose to try to roll it past player E or to throw it to another player. If player A throws the ball to another player, player E must slide step around the small grid to defend.
5. Play continues with players A through D either attempting to roll the ball past player E or throwing the ball to another player.
6. If a player succeeds in rolling the ball past player E, they exchange places.

This is a fun drill with lots of opportunities for sliding to get to rolling balls. Encourage players on the sides of the large grid to make quick decisions about whether to roll the ball or to throw to another player. This keeps the player in the middle moving and will eventually create a space for the ball to be rolled through the small grid. Use a safety ball for beginning players and a baseball for intermediate players.

19. Crossover Fielding 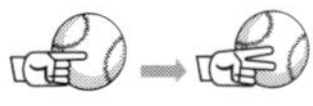

Purpose: To develop the crossover fielding technique.

Number of Players: 2
Equipment: 1 safety ball or baseball, 2 game markers
Time: 5 to 7 minutes

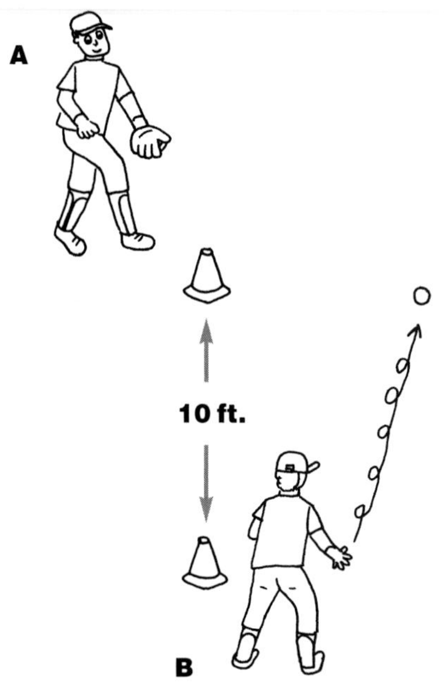

1. Place two game markers 10 feet apart.
2. Position a player beside each marker.
3. Player B rolls a ball to the opposite side of player A's game marker.
4. Player A uses a crossover step to move to a position to field the ball.
5. Player A fields the ball and rolls it to the opposite side of player B's game marker.
6. Player B uses a crossover step to move to a position to field the ball.
7. Repeat.

The crossover step is used to move to the ball quickly when it is too far away to use the slide step successfully. To execute the crossover step, pivot on the foot closest to the direction of the ball while crossing the other foot over top of the pivoting foot with a long stride. Use a safety ball for beginning players and a baseball for intermediate players. To challenge intermediate players, increase the distance between the markers and have the players throw bouncing balls instead of rolling ones.

When fielding ground balls, players should be low to the ground with their legs and hips flexed.

20. Partner Ground Ball Game 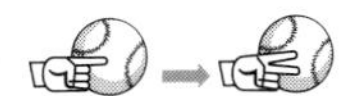

Purpose: To develop technique for fielding ground balls.

Number of Players: 2
Equipment: 1 safety ball or baseball, 2 game markers
Time: 5 to 7 minutes

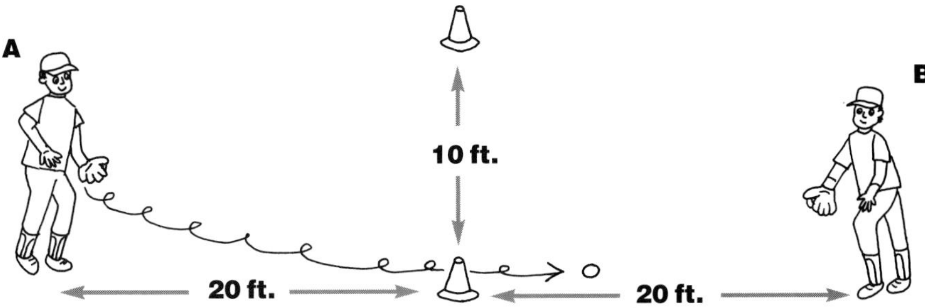

1. Place two game markers 10 feet apart.
2. Position players 20 feet on each side of an imaginary line between the two markers.
3. Player A rolls a ground ball to player B. If player B fields the ball, he earns 1 point.
4. Player B rolls a ground ball to player A. If player A fields the ball, she earns 1 point.
5. Players continue rolling ground balls to each other. The first player to earn 20 points wins.

This drill gives players lots of repetitions fielding ground balls. Instruct players to begin in a ready position, to move to the ball quickly using a slide or crossover step, and to play the ball in front of them whenever possible. Encourage players to watch the ball into their glove. Players should throw a variety of ground balls, including slow rollers, one-hoppers, and two-hoppers. Use a safety ball for beginning players and a baseball for intermediate players.

21. Ground Ball Relay

Purpose: To develop technique for fielding ground balls.

Number of Players: 8
Equipment: 2 baseballs, 4 game markers
Time: 8 to 10 minutes

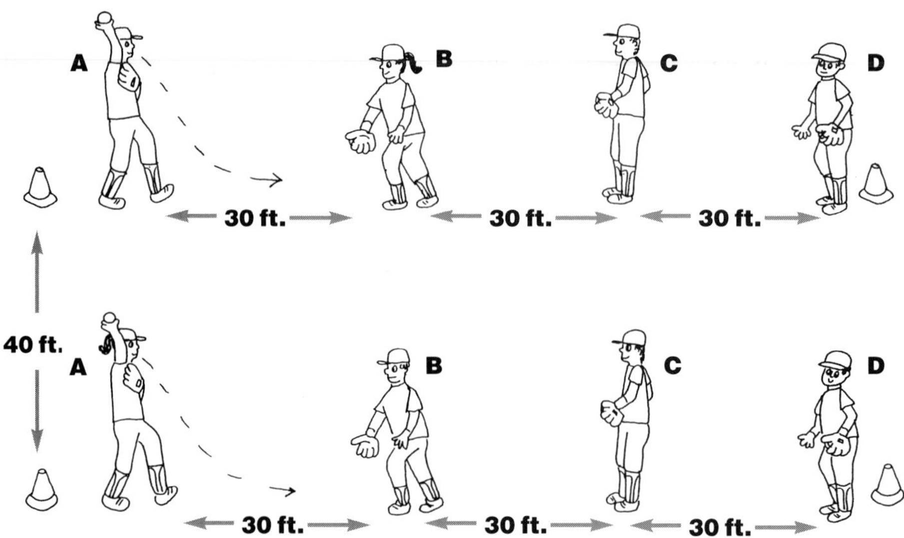

1. Position two game markers 90 feet apart. Position the other two game markers, also 90 feet apart, 40 feet from the first set.
2. Divide players into two teams of four.
3. Position each team on an imaginary line between a set of game markers. Team members should be 30 feet apart.
4. On a coach's signal, player A on each team throws a ground ball to player B.
5. Player B fields the ground ball and throws a ground ball to player C.
6. Player C fields the ball and throws a ground ball to player D.
7. Player D catches the ball and throws a ground ball back to player C.
8. Repeat until player A has the ball.
9. The first team finished wins.

Encourage players to be in a ready position and to watch the ball into their glove. The more repetition players experience, the better chance they have to develop their skills. This drill can be modified to accommodate more players, used as part of station work, or used in the outfield when the infield is being used for other activities.

22. Partner Two-Grid Ground Ball Game

Purpose: To develop technique for fielding ground balls.

Number of Players: 4
Equipment: 1 baseball, 6 game markers
Time: 12 to 15 minutes

1. Use four game markers to make a 50-by-10-foot rectangular grid. Position another two game markers to mark the middle of the grid's longer sides.
2. Position player A1 on an imaginary line between the middle markers. Position players B1 and B2 at one end of the grid and player A2 at the opposite end.
3. Player B1 stands behind the end markers of the grid, trying to throw a ground ball between the middle markers past player A1. If successful, player B1 earns 1 point.
4. If player A1 prevents the ball from going between the markers, no points are scored.
5. If the ball goes past player A1, player A2 retrieves it and throws it back to player A1. Player A1 then throws it back to player A2 and takes a position between the end markers. Player B1 takes a position between the middle markers.
6. Player A2, standing behind the end line of the grid, tries to throw the ball past player B1.
7. The game continues with players on each team changing roles fielding between the middle markers and throwing from the end line.
8. Whichever team scores 10 points first wins.

Encourage fielders to stay in front of the ball by using the slide step when appropriate and the crossover step when necessary. Throwers should deliver a variety of bouncing balls to the right and left of the fielder in the middle.

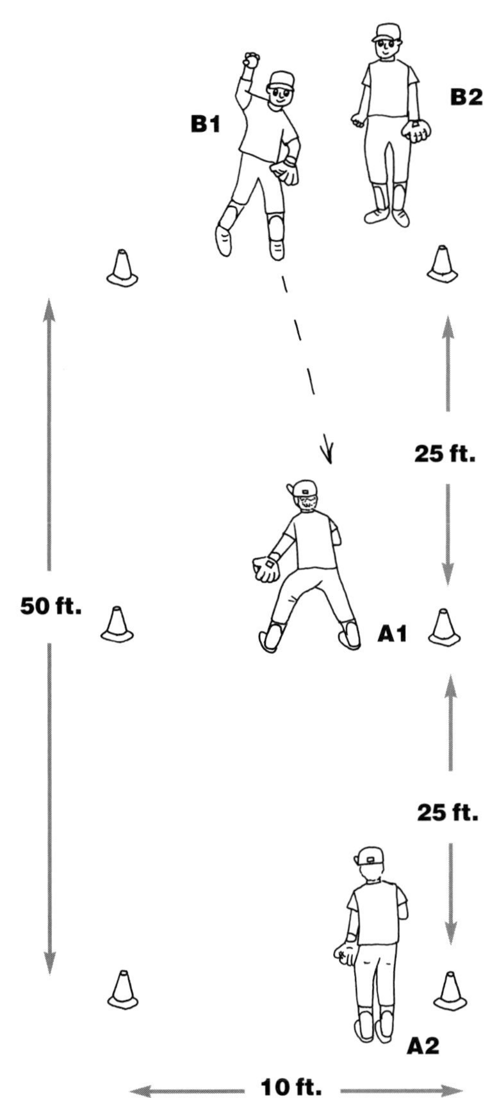

23. Developing the Crow-Hop 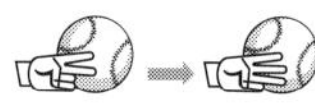

Purpose: To develop the crow-hop technique.

Number of Players: 4
Equipment: 1 baseball, 4 game markers
Time: 5 to 7 minutes

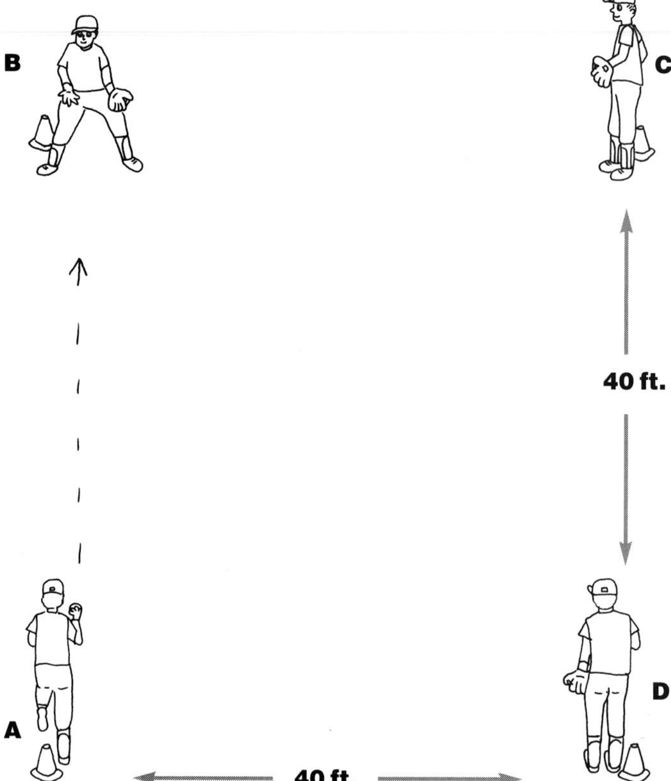

1. Use four game markers to make a 40-by-40-foot grid.
2. Position one player on each corner of the grid.
3. Player A executes a crow-hop and throws to player B.
3. Player B catches the ball, crow-hops, and throws to player C.
4. Player C catches, crow-hops, and throws to player D.
5. Player D catches, crow-hops, and throws to player A.
6. Repeat.

The crow-hop is a way to generate momentum in the direction of a throw to help players throw with greater speed. To execute the crow-hop, players step forward with the nondominant foot, slide the dominant foot toward the nondominant foot, lift the nondominant foot, and then step forward while pushing off with the dominant foot and throwing. This step-together-step action should be used when greater throwing velocity is needed and players have time to make the foot movement.

24. Three-Person Rolling 

Purpose: To develop the charging technique for fielding ground balls.

Number of Players: 3
Equipment: 1 baseball, 2 game markers
Time: 5 to 7 minutes

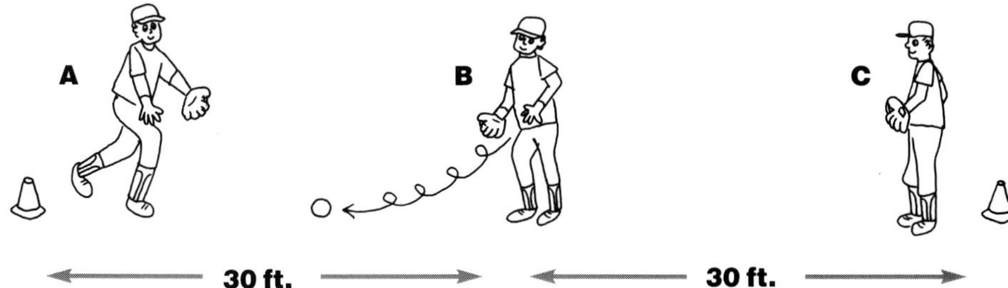

1. Place two game markers 60 feet apart.
2. Position a player at each end of an imaginary line between the game markers.
3. Position the third player halfway between the first two players. Players should be 30 feet apart.
4. Player B slowly rolls the ball to player A.
5. Player A charges the ball, fields it, and runs a few steps toward player C before rolling the ball to him.
6. While player A's throw is in motion, player B trades places with player A.
7. Player C charges the ball, fields it, and runs a few steps toward player B before rolling the ball to her.
8. Repeat.

This is a fast-paced drill with lots of action. Encourage players to charge the ball quickly. When fielding balls that must be charged, players should flex their legs and hips to help lower their upper body.

25. Charging Ground Balls

Purpose: To develop technique for fielding ground balls that are moving slowly.

Number of Players: 5
Equipment: 1 baseball, 4 game markers
Time: 5 to 7 minutes

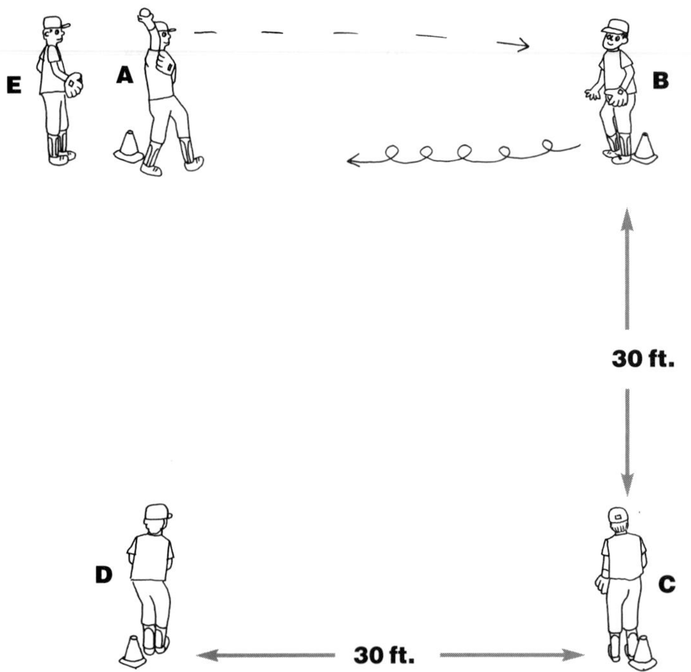

1. Use four game markers to make a 30-by-30-foot grid.
2. Position a player at each corner of the grid.
3. Position a fifth player (E) outside the corner occupied by player A.
4. Player A throws the ball to player B.
5. Player B rolls the ball slowly toward player A.
6. Player A charges the ball, fields it, and tosses it back to player B.
7. Player A moves to the corner where player B started. Player E occupies the corner where player A started.
8. Player B throws the ball to player C. Player C rolls the ball slowly back toward player B, who charges the ball, fields it, and tosses it to player C.
9. Player C throws the ball back to player D. Player D rolls the ball slowly back toward player C, who charges the ball, fields it, and tosses it to player D. Player D then repeats the action with player E.
10. Repeat action so that players end up moving all the way around the grid several times.

Players must understand that balls traveling at different speeds require different reactions on their part. In this case, the ball is moving slowly so they must charge the ball. Encourage players to charge the ball quickly. As they field the ball, they should be low to the ground with their legs and hips flexed.

26. Twenty-One Fielding

Purpose: To improve fielding reflexes.

Number of Players: 4
Equipment: 1 baseball, 1 fungo bat
Time: 10 to 12 minutes

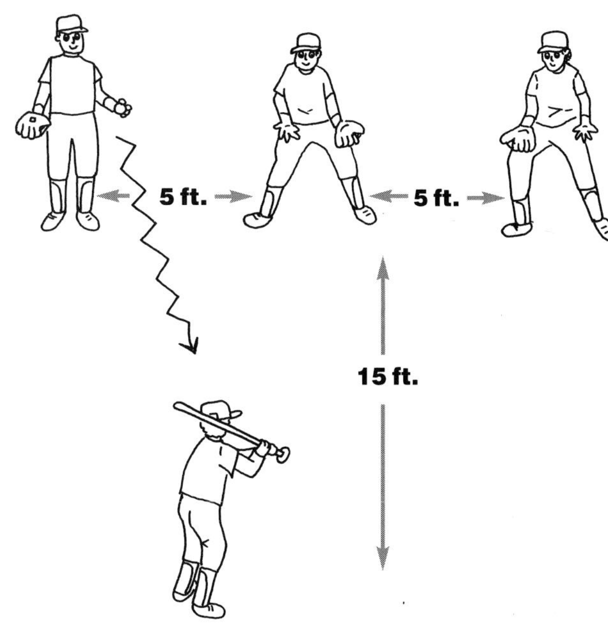

1. Position three players 5 feet apart in a line. One player has a baseball.
2. Position the fourth player with a fungo bat 15 feet from the line of players.
3. The player with the ball tosses it to the fungo hitter, who strikes the ball to one of the players in the line.
4. If a fielder catches a ground ball, the fielding team earns 1 point. A ball caught in the air earns 5 points.
5. If the fungo hitter hits the ball between the players, the fielders lose all of their points and the game starts over.
6. If the fungo hitter hits a ball over a fielder, the hitter is automatically out, the game starts over, and the players rotate.
7. If a fielder makes an error, the fielders lose all of their points, the game starts over, and the fielder who made the error moves to the extreme left of the line.
8. When the fielding team reaches 21 points, the game ends and the fungo hitter goes to the left side of the line. The player on the extreme right of the line becomes the new fungo hitter.

Before starting this drill, instruct players how to "choke up" on the bat to play a pepper-type game (a fast-moving, hitting and fielding game). This will reduce the chance of injury. Encourage players to maintain a ready position at all times.

27. Fly Ball Circle

Purpose: To develop technique for catching fly balls from a stationary position.

Number of Players: 5
Equipment: 1 safety ball
Time: 8 to 10 minutes

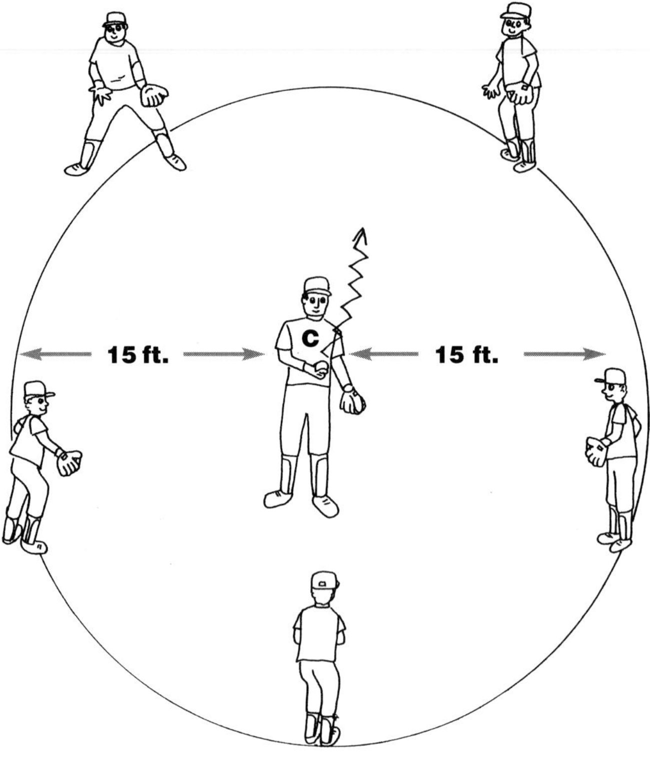

1. Position players in a 30-foot-diameter circle.
2. A coach stands in the middle of the circle.
3. The coach tosses a ball 6 to 8 feet above the head of one of the players so that the player doesn't have to move to catch it.
4. The coach repeats the action with another player but in no particular order.
5. If a player makes the catch, she earns 2 points for the team. If a player does not make the catch, the coach earns 1 point.
6. Whoever earns 10 points first—the coach or the team—wins.

Instruct players to be in a ready position. As the ball is tossed, players should "track" the ball (follow its pathway with their eyes). Before beginning the drill, demonstrate how to move the glove from below the waist in a ready position to above the shoulders, with the fingers of the glove pointed upward and the glove open.

Making a game out of this activity helps keep players focused and allows them to have fun while they learn. Always reward beginning players more points for being successful (2 points for catching as opposed to the coach's receiving 1 point if the ball is not caught) because their skills are still inconsistent at this level.

28. Fly Ball Grid

Purpose: To develop technique for catching fly balls.

Number of Players: 4

Equipment: 1 safety ball or baseball, 8 game markers

Time: 10 to 12 minutes

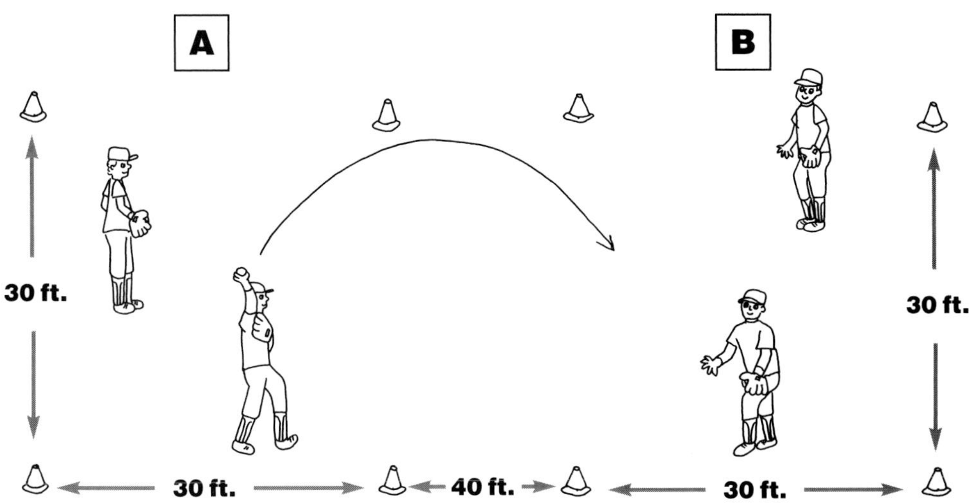

1. Make two 30-by-30-foot grids using four game markers each. The grids should be 40 feet apart.
2. Position two players in each grid.
3. A player in grid A throws a ball in the air so that it can be caught somewhere in grid B.
4. If the ball is caught by a player in grid B, that player throws it in the air so that it can be caught somewhere in grid A.
5. If a ball is dropped or if it lands in one of the grids, the opposite team earns 2 points.
6. If a ball lands outside one of the grids, the opposite team earns 1 point.
7. The first team to earn 10 points wins.

Encourage players to move quickly to the direction of the ball and then slow down the last couple of steps. This slowing action allows them to concentrate on catching the ball without the excess head movement caused by running. Instruct players to have their fingers pointed upward, glove open, watching the ball into their glove. They must communicate with their partners to avoid collisions caused by both players trying to catch the ball at the same time. Use a safety ball for beginning players and a baseball for intermediate players.

29. Fielder Communication 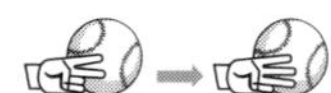

Purpose: To improve communication skills between players on balls that are hit in the air.

Number of Players: 4
Equipment: 1 tennis ball, 1 tennis racket, 4 game markers
Time: 10 to 12 minutes

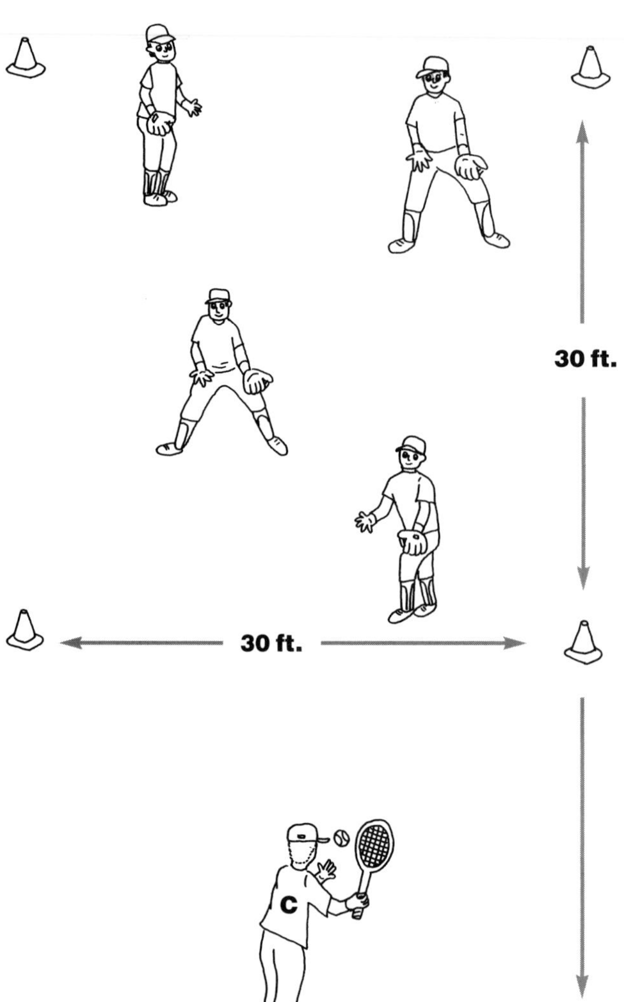

1. Use four game markers to make a 30-by-30-foot grid.
2. Position players in the grid.
3. A coach stands 30 feet from the grid and strikes a ball in the air above the grid.
4. One of the players communicates to the other players his intentions to field the ball by calling out, "I've got it."
5. The fielding player catches the ball and throws it back to the coach.
6. Repeat several times.

Some players are naturally more aggressive than others. All players need to understand, however, that balls hit in another player's space should be fielded by that player. This drill helps players to recognize other players' spaces and to respect other players' rights to field balls in those spaces. Communication developed between players in small-group work leads to better communication between players during full-field games, which helps reduce the possibility of injury while improving the quality of play.

30. Infield Communication 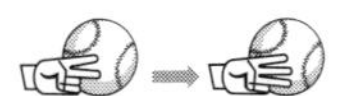

Purpose: To improve communication on pop-ups to the infield.

Number of Players: 5
Equipment: 1 tennis ball, 1 tennis racket
Time: 12 to 15 minutes

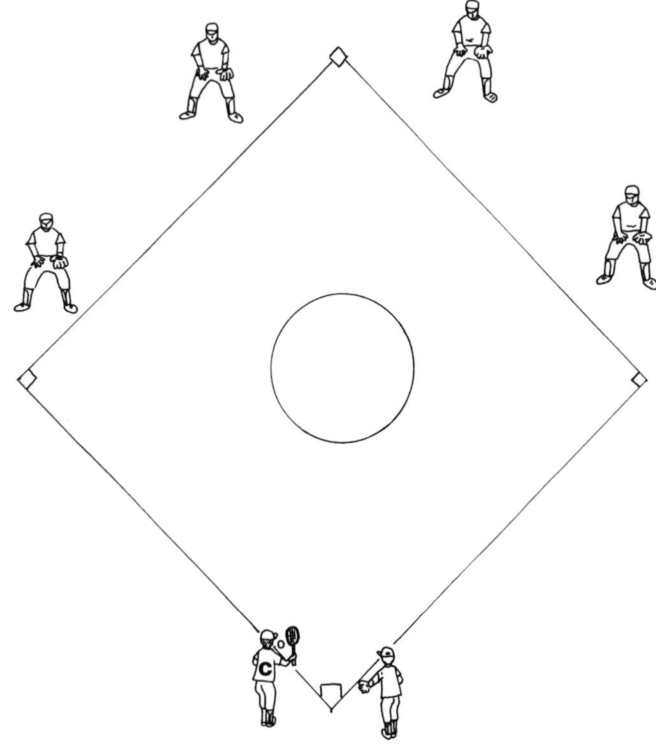

1. Position four players as infielders, one each at first, second, third base, and shortstop.
2. A fifth player acts as catcher for a coach standing at home plate.
3. The coach strikes a tennis ball into the air.
4. One of the infielders communicates "I've got it" to the rest of the players, fields the ball, and returns it to the coach.
5. Repeat.

The coach should place hit balls between players so that players must decide who will field the ball. Instruct players that the shortstop calls off the third-base player for balls hit between them, the second-base player calls off the first-base player for balls hit between them, and the shortstop calls off the second-base player for balls hit between them. The term "call off" means that the player has the authority over the other player to make the catch, so if the shortstop and the second-base player both call for a pop-up hit between them, the second-base player should give way to the shortstop.

31. Fly Ball Partner

Purpose: To develop technique for catching fly balls while moving.

Number of Players: 4
Equipment: 1 baseball, 4 game markers
Time: 8 to 10 minutes

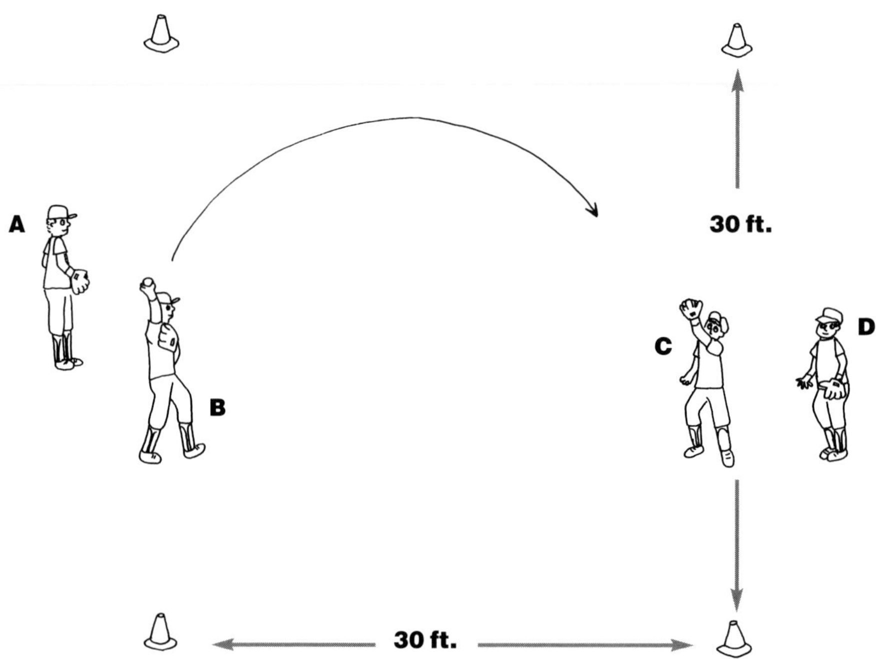

1. Use game markers to make a 30-by-30-foot grid.
2. Position two players at one end of the grid and two others at the opposite end.
3. Player B throws a fly ball toward player C somewhere between the markers on the opposite side of the grid.
4. Player C catches the ball and tosses it to player D.
5. Player D throws a fly ball toward player B. Player D then switches with player C.
6. Player B catches the ball and tosses it to player A. Player A throws a fly ball toward player D then switches with player B.
7. Repeat.

After players have developed the technique for catching fly balls from a stationary position, challenge them by adding movement. Catching fly balls that the player has to move to get to presents a more gamelike situation. Encourage players to move quickly to the direction of the ball and then slow their movement while making the catch, whenever possible.

32. Wall Work 

Purpose: To develop reflexes and decision-making skills for fielding balls in the air and on the ground.

Number of Players: 1
Equipment: 1 rubber baseball
Time: 12 to 15 minutes

1. Position the player 10 feet in front of a rebound wall.
2. Present the player with a series of skill challenges that are designed progressively from easiest to hardest. An example of a series that might be used follows.

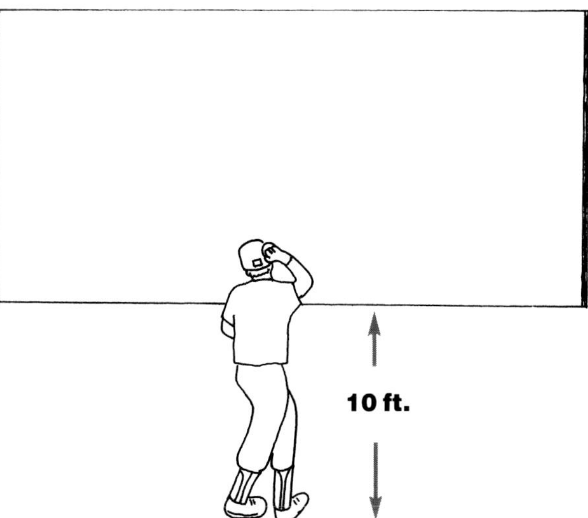

- throw the ball and catch it before it hits the ground
- catch it on one hop
- catch it on two hops
- catch it backhand
- catch it backhand on one hop

This is a drill players can use as homework. They don't need anyone else to work on improving their skills; all they need is some type of ball. If a friend is available, they can make a game out of it. For example, they could each take 10 turns catching the ball backhand on one hop. The one with the most catches wins. To vary the difficulty, instruct the players to stand different distances from the wall.

33. Infield Ground Balls

Purpose: To develop the infielder's fielding and throwing skills.

Number of Players: 8
Equipment: 4 baseballs, 2 fungo bats
Time: 12 to 15 minutes

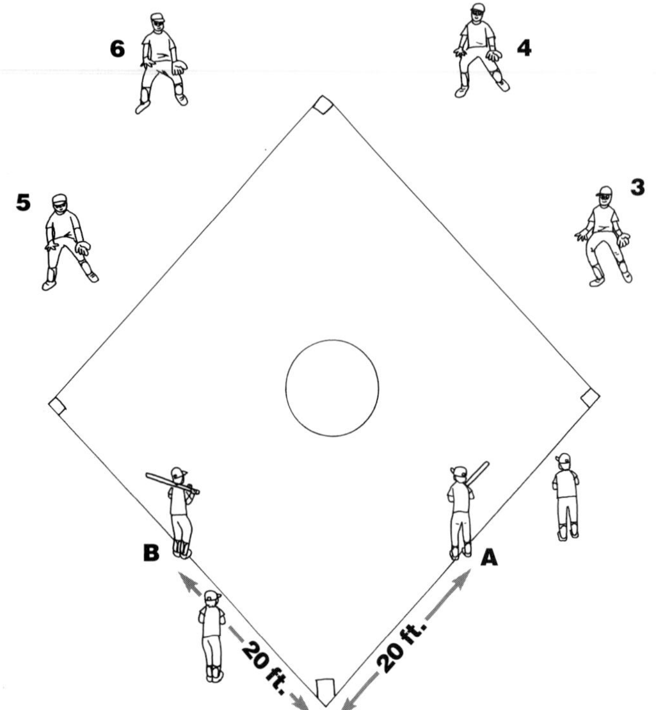

1. Position a player with a fungo bat on each foul line, 20 feet from home plate.
2. Position a player next to each fungo batter to catch thrown balls from infielders.
3. Position a first-, second-, and third-base player and a shortstop at their fielding positions.
4. Both fungo hitters hit ground balls at the same time:
   - Fungo hitter A hits to the shortstop, who throws to first base. The first-base player throws to the catcher for fungo hitter A. Fungo hitter B hits to the second-base player, who throws to third. The third-base player throws to the catcher for fungo hitter B.
   - Fungo hitter A hits to the shortstop, who throws to third. The third-base player throws to the catcher for fungo hitter B. Fungo hitter B hits to the second-base player, who throws to first. The first-base player throws to the catcher for fungo hitter A.
   - Fungo hitter A hits to the third-base player, who throws to first. The first-base player throws to the catcher for fungo hitter B. Fungo hitter B hits to the second-base player, who throws to the shortstop. The shortstop throws to the catcher for fungo hitter A.
   - Fungo hitter A hits to the first-base player, who throws to third. The third-base player throws to the catcher for fungo hitter A. Fungo hitter B hits to the shortstop, who throws to second. The second-base player throws to the catcher for fungo hitter B.

This drill provides lots of repetitions for developing fielding and throwing skills. Encourage players to move in a position in front of the ball when fielding instead of playing the ball to the side.

CHAPTER 5

Fielding by Position Drills

When your players have mastered general fielding skills, it is time to teach position—as well as situation-specific fielding skills. This chapter presents activities to help develop certain techniques used by fielders to defend against batted balls and/or special situations that occur during the game. These special situations occur because of a failure to execute a skill properly (e.g., a pitcher throws a wild pitch) or as a result of an opponent's strategy (e.g., stealing a base). Because of their degree of difficulty, most of the drills designed for this chapter are appropriate for intermediate and advanced players.

It would be impossible to include every possible scenario for each position, so I have selected the ones that occur most frequently (e.g., defending against the bunt and the steal). Small-group drills for holding runners on base, footwork for double plays, how to back up bases, how to deal with balls in the air on sunny days, and how to cope with outfield fences are also included. Such fielding techniques as glove position by infielders, various ready positions for infielders and outfielders, and ways to improve the pitcher's fielding reflexes are presented in a variety of small- and large-group activities.

Many of the activities designed for this chapter can be included as part of batting practice or through small-group station work using assistant coaches to demonstrate, observe and correct, and supervise. This enables you to keep the players moving, with lots of opportunities to gain the valuable experience that will improve their play, help them form good habits, and improve their self-esteem while promoting teamwork.

34. Pitcher Square-Up 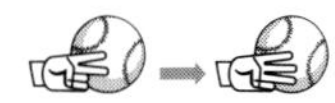

Purpose: To develop the pitcher's fielding reflexes.

Number of Players: 3
Equipment: 2 baseballs
Time: 8 to 10 minutes

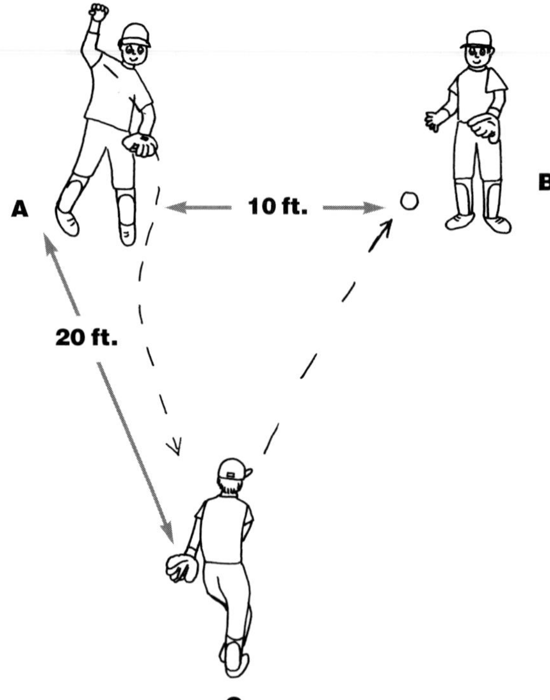

1. Position three players in a triangle so that two players are 10 feet apart and the third is 20 feet from them.
2. Player A and player C (the pitcher 20 feet from the others) hold one ball each; player B does not.
3. Player C winds up and throws his ball to player B.
4. Player A immediately throws a ground ball to player C, who fields it.
5. Player C winds up and throws his ball to player A.
6. Player B immediately throws a ground ball to player C.
7. Repeat several times and then change roles.

Pitchers must learn to deliver a pitch and then get their body in balance by quickly squaring up with their feet parallel and their glove ready. Make this drill either more challenging by shortening the distance between players or less challenging by lengthening the distance.

35. Shinburger 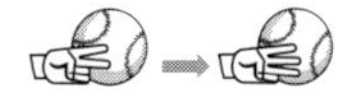

Purpose: To develop the pitcher's fielding skills.

Number of Players: 2
Equipment: 2 safety balls or baseballs, 1 fungo bat
Time: 5 to 7 minutes

1. Position a pitcher 30 feet from a catcher.
2. Position a coach 6 feet to the left of the catcher.
3. The pitcher winds up and throws to the catcher.
4. Just before the pitcher releases the ball, the coach hits a ground ball to the pitcher.
5. The catcher tosses the thrown ball from the pitcher to the coach. The pitcher uses the ball he fielded to repeat the action.

The pitcher must square his body to the home plate and assume a fielding position as quickly as possible. This helps the pitcher become a better fielder and helps protect him from possible injury from balls hit directly at him. For intermediate players, use safety balls to prevent injury.

Note key to symbols, page 21

36. Pitcher Covering First 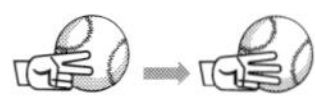

Purpose: To improve the pitcher's technique for covering first base.

Number of Players: 7
Equipment: 2 baseballs, 1 fungo bat
Time: 12 to 15 minutes

1. Position three players as catcher, first-base player, and second-base player in their defensive positions.
2. Position one pitcher on the mound in a ready position and three others on the infield grass awaiting their turn.
3. The first pitcher throws a ball to the catcher.
4. As the ball is thrown, a coach at home plate hits a ground ball to the first- or second-base player.
5. The pitcher runs to cover first base.
6. The pitcher returns the ball to the next pitcher in line and then moves to the end of the line of pitchers.
7. Repeat.

Whenever the ball is hit to the right side, the catcher hollers to the pitcher, "Get over there." If the first-base player fields the ball and can make the play herself, she indicates this to the pitcher. If the first-base player is going away from first base to field the ball, the pitcher needs to cover the base. He does so by running in a pathway similar to a J, meaning he runs toward the first-base line, then angles his run to the base. This allows him to field the throw to first base while moving in the same direction as the base runner, which helps prevent collisions. When there are runners on base, instruct the pitcher to hit first base with his right foot and turn in toward the infield to see if there is another opportunity for a play. When throwing to the pitcher covering first base, the fielder should show the ball early and use an underhand toss when possible.

37. Pitcher Fielding Bunt 

Purpose: To develop the pitcher's technique for fielding bunts.

Number of Players: 7
Equipment: 2 baseballs
Time: 12 to 15 minutes

1. Position three players as catcher, first-base player, and third-base player in their fielding positions.
2. Position four pitchers on the mound with one in a ready position and the other three awaiting their turn.
3. Imaginary runners are on first and second base.
4. The pitcher throws a ball to the catcher from the set position.
5. A coach at home plate rolls a ball, simulating a bunt.
6. The pitcher fields the bunt, listening for the catcher's direction, and throws to the base indicated by the catcher.
7. The catcher throws the pitched ball to the coach while the fielder whom the pitcher threw the bunted ball to throws the ball to the next pitcher.
8. Repeat.

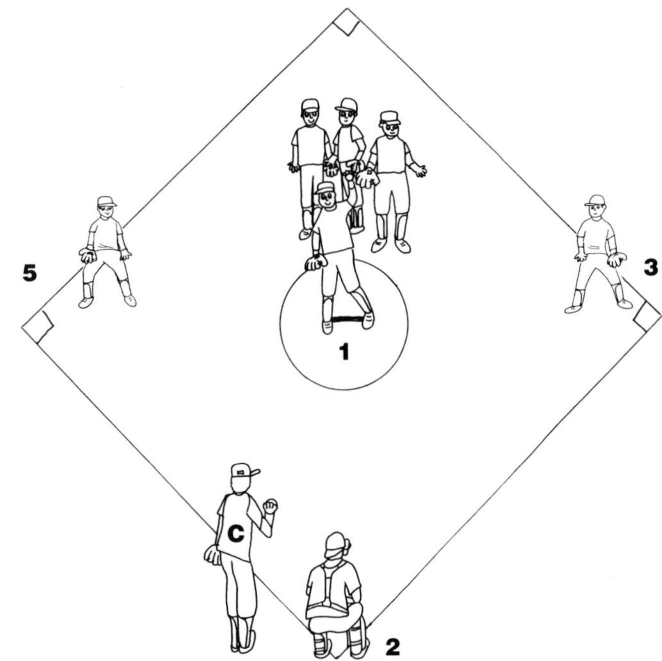

When fielding a bunt, the pitcher should hustle to the ball as quickly as possible, listening for the catcher's directions. Right-handed pitchers throwing to first base should plant their right foot next to the ball, pick the ball up, and throw while pushing off with the right foot, without taking any extra steps. Left-handed pitchers should circle the ball before planting the left foot and throwing. If the play is to third base, reverse the action, with the right-handed pitcher circling the ball and the left-handed pitcher planting the left foot and throwing.

38. Pitcher to Shortstop Double Play

Purpose: To develop the pitcher's technique for turning a double play using the shortstop.

Number of Players: 8
Equipment: 2 baseballs, 1 fungo bat
Time: 12 to 15 minutes

1. Position three players as shortstop, first-base player, and catcher in their fielding positions. Position a second shortstop on the outfield grass, waiting to take the next turn.
2. Position one pitcher on the mound with a ball, with three other pitchers in the infield grass awaiting their turn.
3. The pitcher turns to the shortstop and tells her that if the ball is hit to the pitcher, he will be throwing to the shortstop.
4. The pitcher comes to a set position and throws his ball to the catcher.
5. The coach hits a ground ball to the pitcher, who fields the ball and throws it to the shortstop.
6. The shortstop throws to first base to complete the double play and then trades places with the other shortstop.
7. The first pitcher moves to the end of the line of pitchers. The first-base player throws the ball to the next pitcher.
8. Repeat.

Encourage pitchers always to communicate before the play begins to reduce confusion. The second-base player has no role in this play. Asking a second-base player to back up second would only distract the pitcher's vision. When delivering the ball to second base, the pitcher takes only one step to throw while leading the shortstop to the base.

39. Pitcher Holding Runner 

Purpose: To develop the pitcher's technique for holding runners on base.

Number of Players: 8
Equipment: 1 baseball, helmets
Time: 12 to 15 minutes

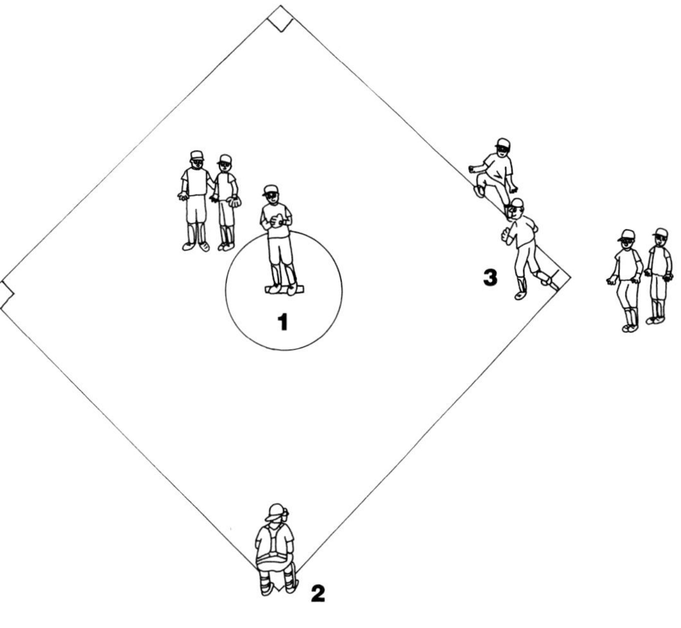

1. Position three base runners at first base, with one ready to take his lead off of first and the other two awaiting their turn.
2. Position three pitchers at the mound, with one by the rubber and the other two awaiting their turn.
3. Position two players as catcher and first-base player in their defensive positions.
4. The pitcher makes contact with the rubber, looking toward home plate.
5. The base runner takes his lead and runs to second base if the ball is delivered to the plate.
6. The pitcher attempts either to pick the runner off if the lead is too great or to disturb the runner's timing by varying the time it takes to deliver the ball to the plate.
7. Rotate in a new pitcher and runner, and repeat.

The pitcher's job is to disturb the runner's rhythm by holding the ball and stepping off the rubber or by throwing quickly to first as the pitcher's arms are coming up or going down before establishing the set position. Practice all of these moves during this drill. One way pitchers can vary the timing of their pickoff throws is to use a number system. They can count from 1 to 20 to themselves and try to throw to first base on a different number each time. For example, the pitcher comes to the stretch position and begins counting; when he reaches 5, he throws to first. The next time he comes to the stretch position and begins counting, he throws to first when he reaches 15. This helps vary the timing of the throws to disturb the runner's rhythm.

40. Pitcher Force Balk 

Purpose: To develop the pitcher's technique for defending the force balk.

Number of Players: 9
Equipment: 1 baseball, 3 helmets
Time: 12 to 15 minutes

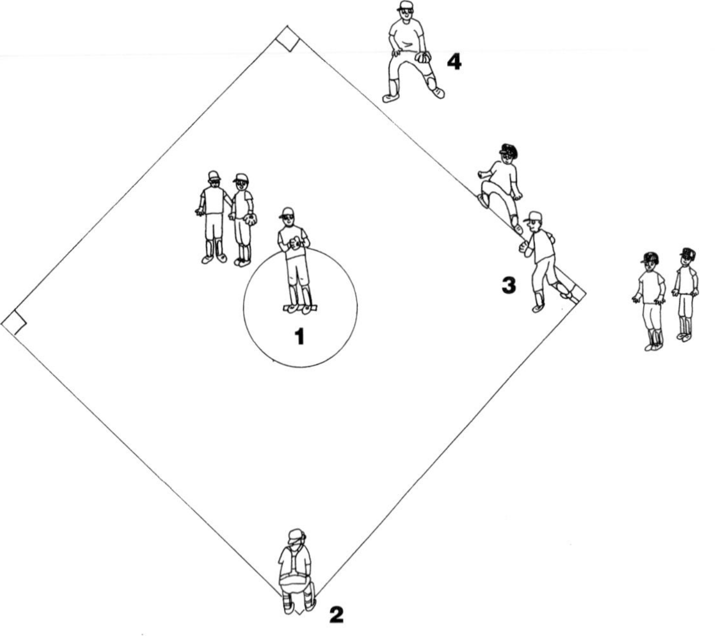

1. Position one base runner at first base, with two others outside the first-base coach's box awaiting their turn.
2. Position a first-base player, second-base player, and catcher in their defensive positions.
3. Position one pitcher on the mound, with two others on the infield grass awaiting their turn.
4. The pitcher makes contact with the rubber.
5. The base runner takes her lead as the pitcher is about to move into the set position.
6. As the pitcher raises his arms to move into the set position, the base runner takes off for second base.
7. The pitcher steps back off the rubber and throws directly to the second-base player, who has moved into the base path after seeing the runner break for second base.
8. The second-base player tags the runner or gets her in a rundown.
9. The pitcher moves to first base to be part of the rundown, if necessary.
10. Repeat with a new pitcher and base runner.

The pitcher should step directly backward off the rubber to make the play. Any movement to first base without throwing the ball is a balk. Any forward motion to the plate before then throwing to second also is a balk. Communication from the first-base player that the runner is stealing also helps the pitcher react faster.

41. Pitcher Pitchout 

Purpose: To develop the pitcher's technique for the pitchout.

Number of Players: 4
Equipment: Catcher's equipment, 1 baseball
Time: 8 to 10 minutes

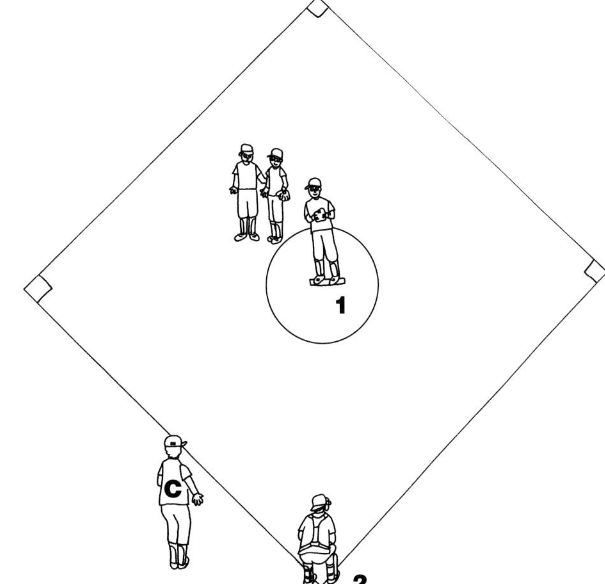

1. Position three pitchers at the mound, with one in a set position and the other two on the infield grass awaiting their turn.
2. Position a catcher in the ready position at a distance appropriate for the players' age group.
3. A coach tells the pitcher whether there is a right- or left-handed batter at the plate. The catcher gives the signal for the pitchout.
4. The pitcher delivers a shoulder-high pitch to the opposite batter's box.
5. Repeat with the next pitcher.

This drill can be executed in the outfield grass. It should be repeated often so that if the situation occurs in a game, players can execute the play routinely. Encourage pitchers to use fastballs in delivering the pitchout. Keeping the ball shoulder high allows the catcher to release the ball faster if a runner is stealing.

42. Phantom Pitcher Backup 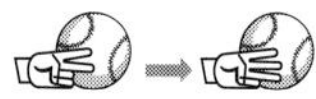

Purpose: To develop the pitcher's technique for backing up bases.

Number of Players: 4
Equipment: None
Time: 8 to 10 minutes

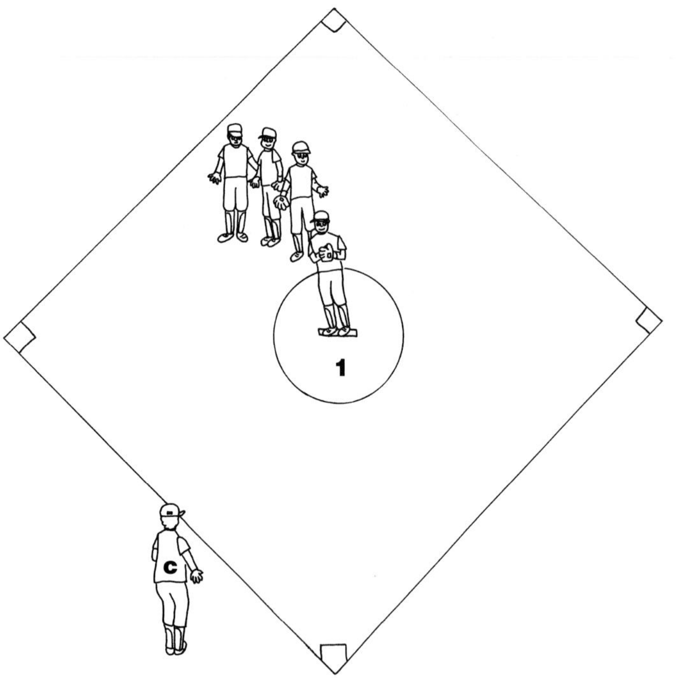

1. Position four pitchers on the mound, with one on the rubber and the others on the infield grass awaiting their turn.
2. A coach calls out the situation, giving the pitcher the number of outs and the location of base runners.
3. The coach tells the pitcher where the ball has been hit.
4. The pitcher reacts by backing up the appropriate base.
5. Repeat with the next pitcher.

The pitcher's work is never done. The game situation dictates where pitchers must go to back up. For base hits to the outfield with no one on base or no possibility of getting the runner out at home, pitchers must back up second base. On all extra-base hits with runners on base, they must go to a position halfway between home and third base to see how the play is developing before making a decision on where to back up. Repetition in drills such as this helps pitchers back up bases in game situations correctly.

43. Pitcher Backup

Purpose: To develop the pitcher's technique for backing up bases.

Number of Players: 15

Equipment: 2 baseballs, 4 helmets, 1 fungo bat

Time: 18 to 20 minutes

1. Position two players as base runners at first and second base. Position two more base runners near first base awaiting their turn.
2. Deploy the defensive team so that all positions are occupied. Position two extra pitchers behind the pitcher's mound on the infield grass awaiting their turn.
3. A coach hits a ground ball or a fly ball to the outfielders.
4. As soon as the ball is hit, the pitcher reacts and moves to a backup position.
5. After the appropriate player fields and returns the ball, a new pitcher steps to the mound and new base runners assume their places at first and second base.
6. Repeat.

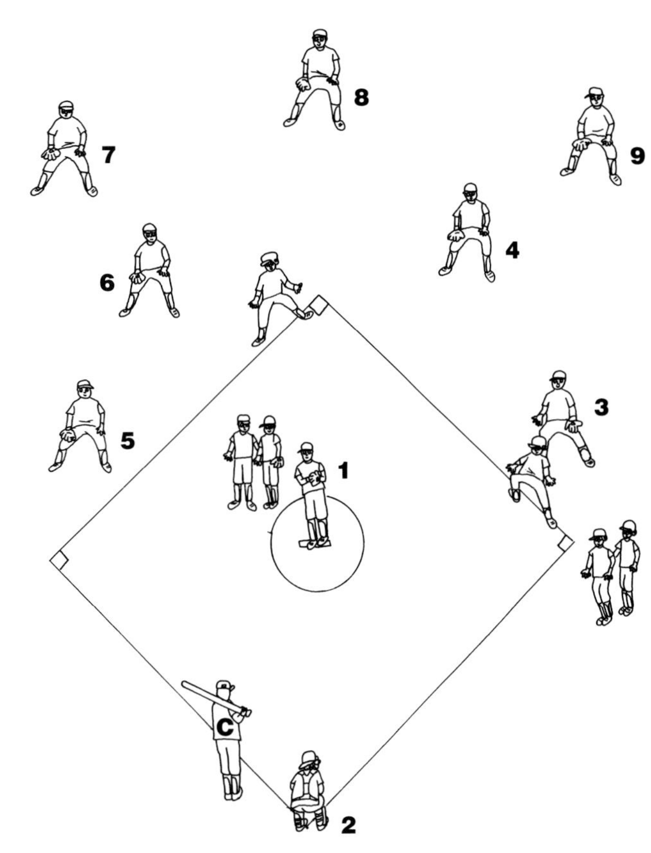

Spend time with individual players in situational activities to help prevent giving up extra bases in game situations. On base hits to the outfield, the pitcher runs to a position behind the third-base line at a point about halfway between home and third base. If he sees that the play will be at home, he runs 30 feet behind home plate—or closer if the backstops won't allow the 30-foot distance. If the play is at third base, he backs up the third-base player at about 30 feet, a distance that allows him to field errant throws at various angles.

44. Catcher Ready Position 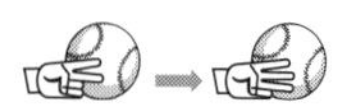

Purpose: To develop the catcher's correct ready position to receive a pitched ball.
Number of Players: 2
Equipment: Catcher's equipment
Time: 3 to 5 minutes

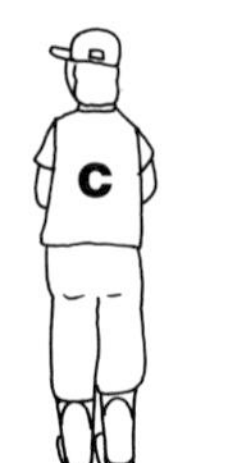

1. Position two catchers side by side.
2. A coach gives these commands: stand, squat, signal, and stance.
3. The coach observes the catchers' position during these phases and makes any necessary corrections.
4. Repeat.

Always conduct the catchers' drills with the catchers wearing all of the equipment. Insist that the catchers protect the signals they are giving by using their glove to shield the view of opponents and by placing their throwing hand closely to their crotch. While catchers are in their stance, their hips should be up and their weight on the soles of their feet, with their throwing hand protected behind them after giving the pitcher the signal.

45. Catcher Backhand 

Purpose: To develop the catcher's backhand technique for receiving outside pitches.
Number of Players: 1
Equipment: Catcher's equipment, 1 baseball
Time: 5 to 7 minutes

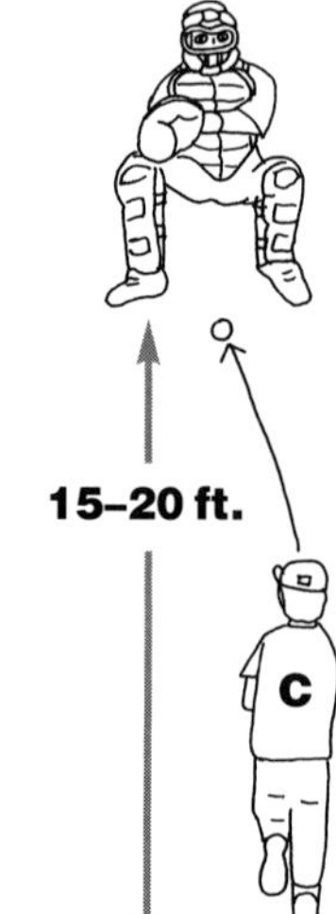

1. Position the catcher near the backstop in a stance ready to receive the ball.
2. A coach positions himself about 15 to 20 feet from the catcher.
3. The coach throws the ball to the outside position of the plate.
4. The catcher crosses the midline of her body with her glove, turning her thumb slightly downward.
5. Repeat several times, occasionally mixing in an inside pitch to keep the catcher honest.

This is a good drill for one-on-one work with a coach. Beginning players have a tendency to turn the thumb of their catching hand upward as they move their glove across the midline of their body. Constant repetition improves this technique. Having more than one baseball available keeps this drill fast-paced.

46. Catcher Backup

Purpose: To develop the catcher's technique for backing up first base.

Number of Players: 5
Equipment: Catcher's equipment, 1 baseball, 1 fungo bat
Time: 8 to 10 minutes

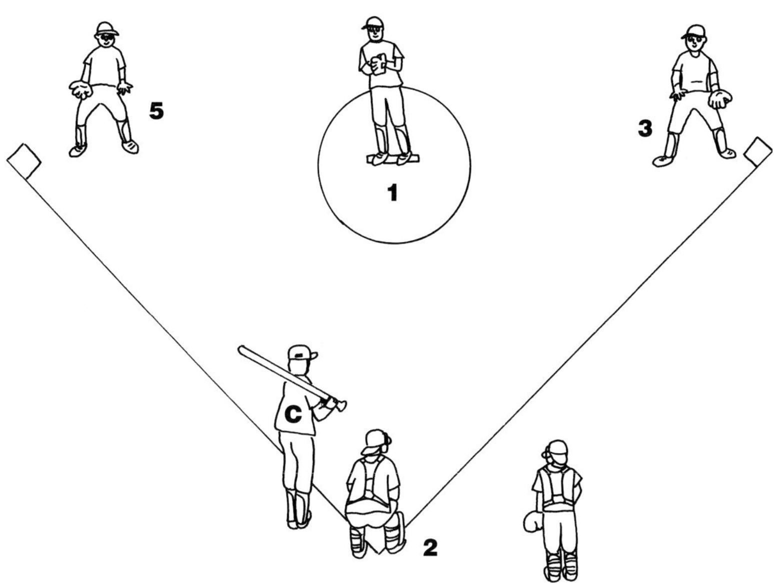

1. Position a catcher, pitcher, third-base player, and first-base player in their fielding positions. Position a second catcher near home plate awaiting his turn.
2. The pitcher throws to the catcher, and a coach immediately hits a ground ball or pop-up or tosses the ball out simulating a bunt.
3. On all ground balls, the catcher runs behind first base and about 20 feet outside the baseline.
4. For all hits or bunts, the appropriate player fields the ball and returns it to the coach
5. After each ground ball, the two catchers switch places.
6. Repeat.

This is a tiring but important drill for catchers. The pop-up and bunt give catchers a break from running down the line on each play. Insist that catchers position themselves far enough outside first base to have a chance of fielding any wild throws. Constant repetition of this drill helps make moving down the first-base line automatic for the catcher when there are no runners on base.

47. Catcher Wild Pitch 

Purpose: To develop the catcher's technique for blocking wild pitches.

Number of Players: 2
Equipment: Catcher's equipment, 1 safety ball or baseball
Time: 5 to 7 minutes

1. Position two catchers close to the backstop.
2. The first catcher assumes his stance (hips up, weight distributed on the soles of his feet, throwing hand protected behind his back).
3. A coach, standing 6 to 8 feet away, throws a ball in the dirt.
4. The first catcher slides to the ball, drops to his knees (elbows by his side, head down), and blocks the ball.
5. The next catcher gets in his stance, and the action is repeated.
6. Continue to alternate catchers. The coach varies the throws, changing the angles of the bounce, the spin, and his distance from the catcher.

Emphasize to catchers the importance of keeping the ball in front so base runners can't advance. Keeping the body slightly cupped and loose instead of straight and rigid helps catchers prevent the ball from bouncing too far away from them. To vary the drill, have catchers begin with their hands behind them and without a glove, allowing them to block the ball only with their body. Use a safety ball initially, until blocking technique improves.

48. Catcher Foul Pop 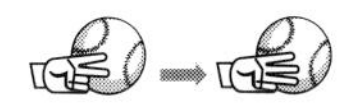

Purpose: To develop the catcher's technique for fielding foul pops.

Number of Players: 2
Equipment: Catcher's equipment, 2 tennis balls, 1 tennis racket
Time: 5 to 7 minutes

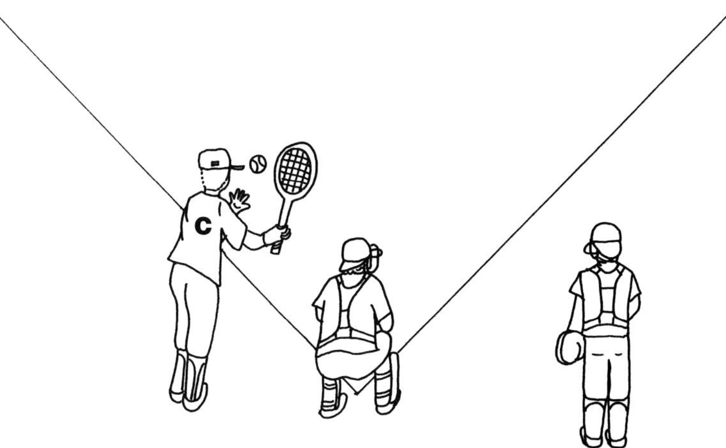

1. Position one catcher at home plate in a stance ready to receive a pitch. Position the other catcher awaiting his turn by the on-deck circle.
2. A coach strikes a tennis ball into the air.
3. The catcher attempts to field the ball.
4. The next catcher steps in, and the action is repeated.
5. The coach varies striking the balls so they travel behind home plate and up the first- and third-base lines. Catchers alternate on each hit.

When fielding foul pops, catchers should move as quickly as possible to the area in which the ball is located, throw their mask in the opposite direction, walk under the ball, and catch it. Taking the mask off improves vision. Throwing the mask in the opposite direction prevents catchers from tripping over it when fielding the ball.

49. Catcher Bunt 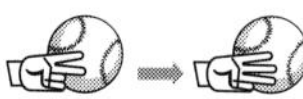

Purpose: To develop the catcher's technique for fielding bunts.

Number of Players: 3
Equipment: Catcher's equipment, 1 baseball
Time: 8 to 10 minutes

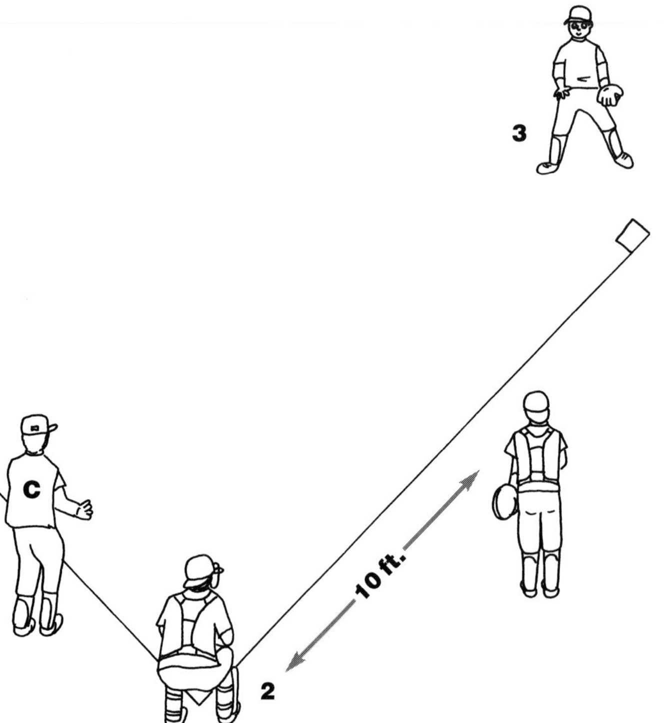

1. Position one player at first base. Position a catcher behind home plate in a ready position to receive a pitch. Position a second catcher 10 feet to the first-base side of home plate awaiting his turn and catching throws from the first-base player.
2. A coach rolls a ball down the first- or third-base line.
3. The first catcher moves from his position behind home plate, fields the ball, and throws it to first base.
4. The first-base player throws the ball to the second catcher, who then gives the ball to the coach and assumes a ready position at home plate to take the next turn fielding the bunt. The first catcher moves to the position along the first-base line vacated by the second catcher.
5. Repeat.

Instruct catchers to pick up the ball and step inside the line when fielding bunts on the first-base side. This helps prevent hitting the base runners with the throw. Left-handed catchers should hustle to the ball while circling it, plant their left foot next to the ball, pick it up, step inside the line, and throw.

When fielding a bunt on the third-base side, left-handed catchers plant their left foot next to the ball, and pick up and throw the ball. Right-handed catchers will circle the ball, plant their right foot next to it, then pick up and throw the ball.

50. Catcher First Base 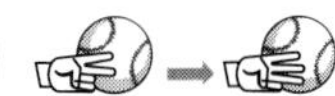

Purpose: To develop the catcher's technique for throwing to first base.

Number of Players: 3

Equipment: Catcher's equipment, 1 baseball

Time: 8 to 10 minutes

1. Position one player at first base.
2. Position a catcher at home plate in a ready position to receive a pitched ball. Position a second catcher in the on-deck circle awaiting her turn.
3. A coach, standing 15 feet in front of home plate, throws the ball to the first catcher.
4. The catcher intentionally drops the ball, simulating a dropped third strike.
5. The catcher picks the ball up, takes two or three steps inside the first-base line, and throws the ball to first base.
6. The first-base player throws the ball to the coach.
7. The catchers trade places.
8. Repeat.

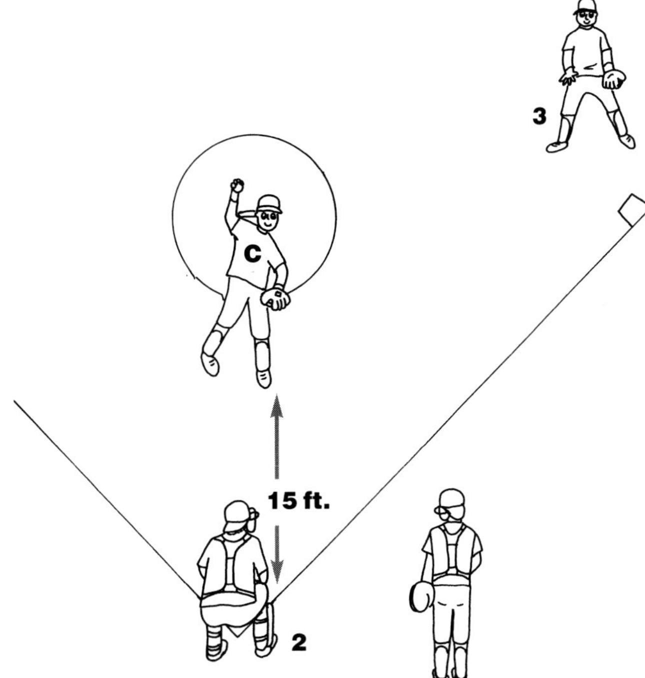

Inexperienced catchers often drop third strikes. Encourage catchers to pick up the ball calmly and throw to first. Walking a couple of steps inside the line helps prevent them from striking the runner with the ball. Placing catchers in this drill helps make this play routine for them should it occur in a game situation.

51. Catcher Stealing 

Purpose: To develop the catcher's technique for throwing during attempts to steal second base.

Number of Players: 7
Equipment: Catcher's equipment, 1 baseball, 3 helmets
Time: 12 to 15 minutes

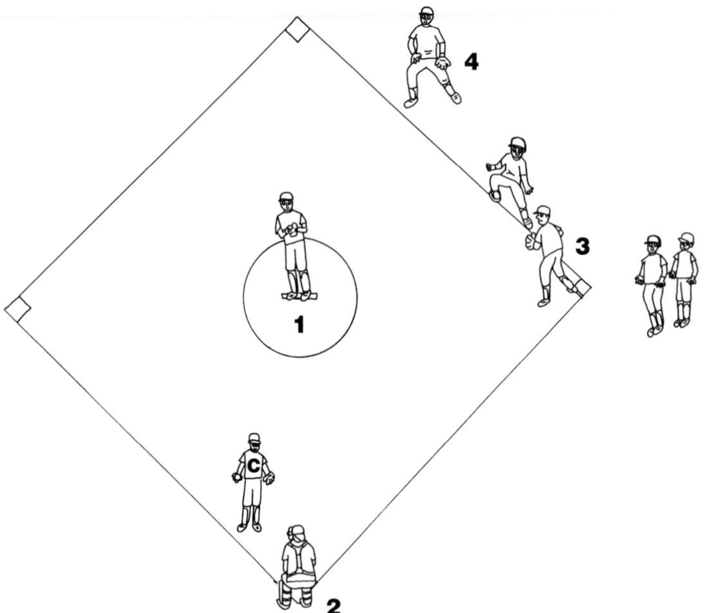

1. Position a first-base player, second-base player, pitcher, and catcher in their defensive positions.
2. Position one base runner at first base and two others off the first-base line awaiting their turn.
3. The runner at first base takes a two-stride lead.
4. A coach, standing in front of the batter's box, throws the ball underhand to the catcher. This is the signal for the base runner to run to second.
5. After receiving the ball, the catcher throws it to second base. The second-base player returns the ball to the coach.
6. The next catcher and base runner take their positions.
7. Repeat several times.
8. Add a player as a batter (who does not swing). Begin the drill again with the pitcher holding the ball in the set position.
9. The pitcher has the option of throwing to first or throwing home. If he throws home, the runner on first breaks for second base and the catcher makes the play.

Encourage catchers to be in a ready position, anticipating the steal, with their hips slightly higher so they will be able to catch, step, and throw. Instruct catchers to use an overhand throw. Sidearm or three-quarter throwing motions cause the ball to curve. Insist that catchers throw the ball to second base, not to a player covering second. If they wait for the player to move to second before they throw, the throw will be late. Inserting the batter in the last part of the drill makes the situation more gamelike by restricting the catcher's vision.

52. Catcher Double Play

Purpose: To develop the catcher's technique for turning double plays.

Number of Players: 5
Equipment: Catcher's equipment, 1 baseball, 1 fungo bat
Time: 8 to 10 minutes

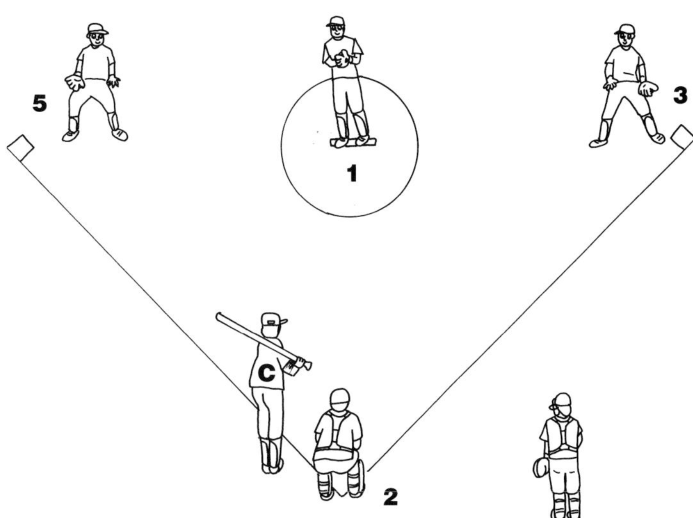

1. Position a pitcher, third-base player, first-base player, and catcher in their defensive positions. Position a second catcher in the on-deck circle to receive throws from the first-base player and to take the next turn.
2. Imaginary runners are on first, second, and third base.
3. A coach hits a ground ball to the pitcher, third-base player, or first-base player, who fields the ball and throws it to the first catcher.
4. The catcher catches the ball while touching home plate and then throws to first.
5. The first-base player throws the ball to the second catcher, waiting in the on-deck circle, who hustles to the plate, gives the ball to the coach, and gets in position to take the next turn.
6. Repeat.

Instruct catchers that for a double-play ball to home plate, they should step in front of the plate and square their shoulders to the player who has fielded the ball. When receiving the ball, they should step toward the ball with their left foot while touching the plate with their right foot. After receiving the ball, they should pivot and throw to first. After their technique improves, add actual base runners to make the drill more gamelike.

53. First-Base Player Footwork

Purpose: To develop the first-base player's footwork for receiving throws from infielders.

Number of Players: 1
Equipment: 1 baseball
Time: 5 to 7 minutes

1. Position the first-base player behind first base and off the foul line at a distance where she can comfortably move to first base in time to receive a throw and get a batter out in a game situation.
2. A coach stands between the pitcher's mound and second base.
3. When the coach raises his hand, the first-base player makes a J-move (uses a bended, or curved, run) to first base to receive the coach's throw.
4. The first-base player throws the ball back to the coach.
5. Repeat.

This is a very simple drill but one that will improve footwork if repeated hundreds of times. The J-move is used so first-base players can move to the base at an angle that allows better balance. Encourage first-base players to move to the base as soon as possible. Some coaches prefer that first-base players only use their dominant foot to contact the base (left-handers use their left foot). I prefer that they straddle the base with their heels making contact. If the ball is thrown inside toward home plate, they contact the base with the right foot and extend with the left. If the ball is thrown to the outfield side, they contact the base with the left foot and extend with the right. Whichever method is used, the first-base player should be fully extended when receiving the ball.

Vary the throws right, left, and in the dirt. For balls in the dirt, first-base players should try to keep a foot on the bag and catch the ball on the short hop (right after it bounces) if they feel there is a chance to get an out. If there is no chance, they should come off the base and block the ball.

54. First-Base Player Holding

Purpose: To develop the first-base player's footwork when holding runners on base.

Number of Players: 6
Equipment: Catcher's equipment, 2 baseballs, 2 helmets, 1 fungo bat
Time: 8 to 10 minutes

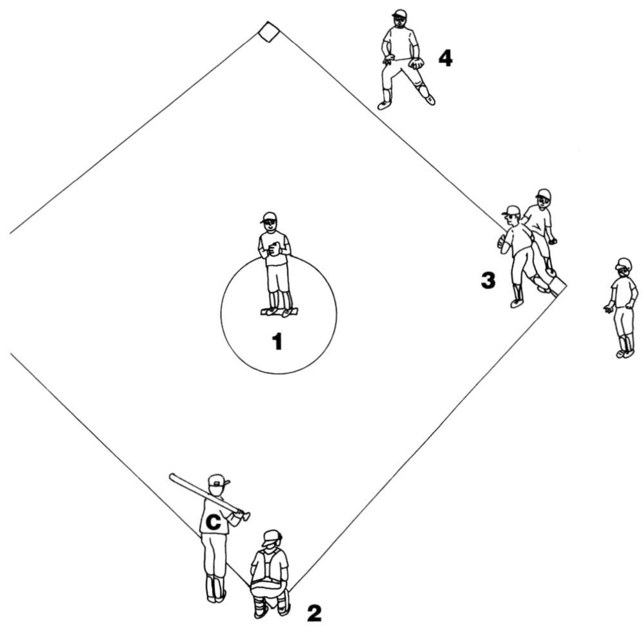

1. Position a first-base player in a position for holding runners on base. The right foot of left-handed players should touch the inside corner of first base closest to home plate. Right-handed players should modify this positioning so that their right foot is at a 45-degree angle to first base and their left foot is pointing toward the pitcher.
2. Position a pitcher, catcher, and second-base player in their fielding positions.
3. Position a runner on first base. Position a second base runner in foul territory awaiting his turn.
4. The pitcher comes to a set position and throws to the catcher at home plate. The catcher receives the ball.
5. As soon as the pitcher begins the move to home plate, the first-base player slides off first base and into fielding position.
6. A coach standing at home plate with another ball hits a ground ball to the pitcher, the second-base player, or the first-base player.
7. When the coach hits the ball, the base runner runs toward second base while the infielders communicate as to who has the ball and who is covering first base. After the play, the base runner jogs back to foul territory on the first-base side to await his next turn.
8. Repeat.

Encourage the pitcher to throw to first base occasionally. Although this isn't a pickoff drill, this action makes the drill more gamelike. This drill assumes that the runner is going and that there is no play at second base. Instruct the first-base player to field as many balls as possible. Ranging toward second base shouldn't present a problem, because the pitcher should be covering first.

55. First-Base Player Bunt 

Purpose: To develop the first-base player's technique for fielding bunts.

Number of Players: 2
Equipment: 3 baseballs
Time: 8 to 10 minutes

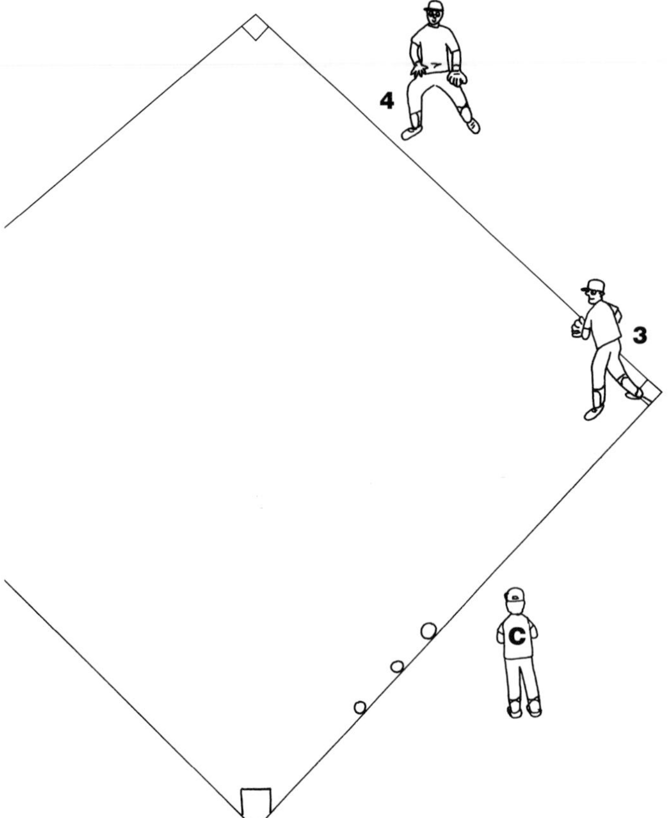

1. Position a first-base player so that he's holding an imaginary runner on base. Position a second-base player at his normal position for a runner at first base.
2. Place three baseballs along the first-base line at varying distances from home base.
3. On a coach's signal, the first-base player charges the ball, plants his dominant foot next to the ball while picking it up, and throws it to the second-base player, who has moved to cover first base.
4. The second-base player stays at first base to receive the next two throws.
5. The first-base player moves to the second and third ball and repeats the action.
6. The coach replaces the balls at different distances.
7. Repeat.

This drill can be performed in the outfield. Encourage first-base player to move to the ball as quickly as possible. By planting the dominant foot (left foot for left-handed players and right foot for right-handed players) next to the ball, players should be able to pick up the ball, push off with the dominant foot, and throw without taking any unnecessary steps. This saves time in executing the play.

56. First-Base Player Pickoff

Purpose: To develop the first-base player's pickoff technique.

Number of Players: 3
Equipment: 1 baseball
Time: 10 to 12 minutes

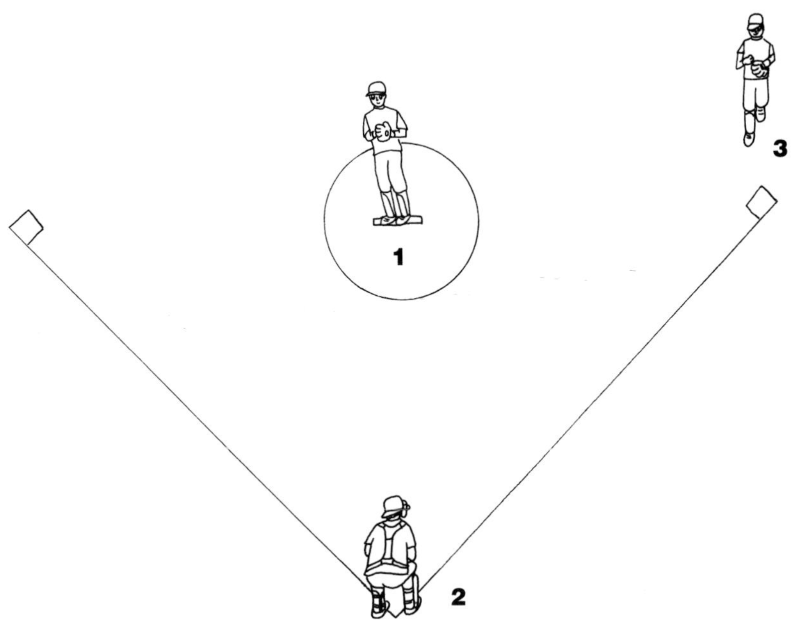

1. Position a first-base player behind an imaginary runner at first base. Position a pitcher and catcher in their normal positions.
2. A coach gives a verbal signal from the bench that the play is on.
3. The first-base player moves slowly and then quickly to the base.
4. The pitcher throws quickly to first. The pitcher knows when to throw because the catcher, who is watching the first-base player, lowers his glove as the signal.
5. Repeat several times.

Begin this drill with imaginary base runners so that infielders can get a feel for the timing involved. Next, add base runners who remain passive to allow for drill execution. As players' skills improve, base runners should react as in a game situation. To make the drill gamelike, place runners at first and second and instruct them to steal if the pitcher throws to the plate. This encourages them to take their best lead off the base. During this gamelike phase, also place other infield defensive players at their positions.

57. Second-Base Player Double-Play Pivot 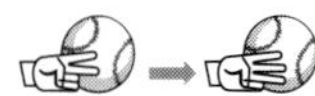

Purpose: To develop the second-base player's double-play pivot.

Number of Players: 1
Equipment: 1 baseball
Time: 12 to 15 minutes

1. Position the second-base player at double-play depth (in a couple of steps toward home and toward second base).
2. Position a coach with a baseball in the area between shortstop and third base.
3. When the coach raises his hand to throw, the second-base player breaks to the base as fast as he can at an angle that allows his shoulders to be square to the coach. As he reaches the base, he slows down for good balance to receive the throw.
4. The second-base player uses a straddle, pivot, or push-off move and makes a phantom throw to first base.
5. Repeat.

This drill provides hundreds of repetitions for the second-base player without having to use other players. It may be done in a section of the outfield. Vary the angle from which the ball is thrown by moving before each throw. Use two second-base players to make the drill more fast-paced and to train another player to play the position in case of injury.

The straddle move should be used when the second-base player has plenty of time to make the play. To execute the straddle, second-base players straddle the base with both feet. As they collect the ball, they lift their left foot, touching the base, and step with the left foot toward first. If a fast runner adds pressure or if the play is on a steal or a hit and run, second-base players may have to pivot or push off to avoid the base runner. If the pivot is used, players hit the base with their left foot (left foot slightly turned toward first), step across the base with their right foot (slightly turned toward first), and make a phantom throw to first. The push-off method is executed by placing the left foot on the base, catching the ball, and pushing backward simultaneously, then planting the right foot and making a phantom throw to first. Practice these moves without base runners to develop footwork and timing.

58. Second-Base Player Double Play 

Purpose: To develop the second-base player's double-play pivot.

Number of Players: 6
Equipment: 2 baseballs, 1 fungo bat
Time: 12 to 15 minutes

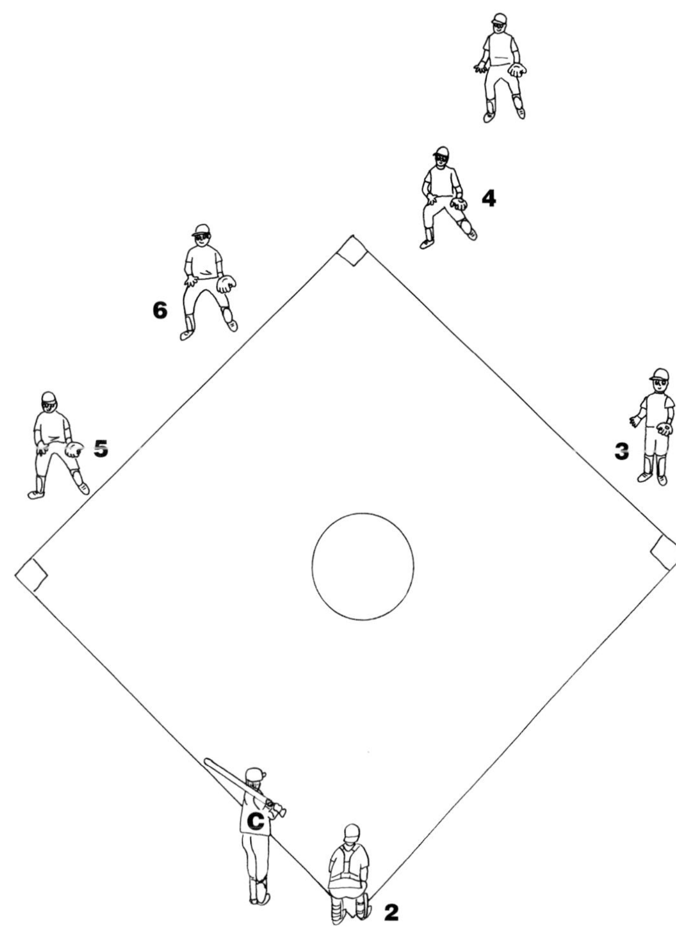

1. Position a third-base player, shortstop, second-base player, and first-base player in their double-play fielding positions. Position a second-base player on the outfield grass to alternate turns.
2. Position a coach at home plate to hit fungoes and another player to catch balls thrown from first base at the conclusion of the double play.
3. The coach randomly hits ground balls to the shortstop and third-base player, who complete a double play.
4. Repeat, alternating second-base players.

Encourage second-base players to vary the footwork at the base to include the straddle, pivot, and push-off steps. To simulate a runner putting pressure on the second-base player, the player catching for the coach at home plate can occasionally yell, "Steal!" This indicates to second-base players that they must execute a move to get out of the path of the base runner. This drill offers second-base players numerous repetitions to receive the throw, pivot, and throw to first. As second-base players become more efficient, add base runners. This drill can easily be incorporated as part of a batting practice.

59. Double-Play Feeding 

Purpose: To develop the double-play feed by the shortstop and second-base player.

Number of Players: 6
Equipment: 2 baseballs, 1 fungo bat
Time: 5 to 7 minutes

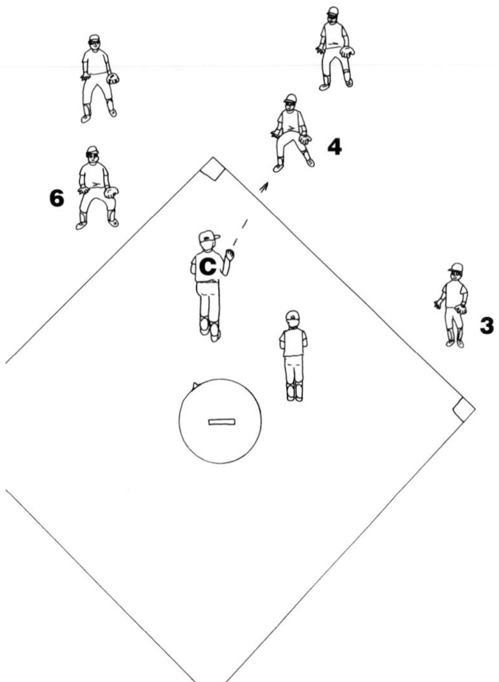

1. Position a shortstop, second-base player, and first-base player at double-play depth. Position a second group of middle infielders awaiting their turn.
2. A coach assumes a position behind the pitcher's mound. Position another player beside the coach to catch balls returned by the first-base player.
3. The coach throws a ball to the second-base player, who feeds the shortstop for a double play. The shortstop throws to first base to complete the double play.
4. The next set of middle infielders repeats the action.
5. The first middle infielders take their original places.
6. The coach throws to the shortstop, who feeds the second-base player for a double play. The second-base player throws to first base to complete the double play.
7. After several rotations, the coach repeats the action but hits a ground ball instead of throwing the ball.
8. Continue, with the coach hitting balls at varying distances from the base.

Allow some time for the middle infielders to work on their feeds without worrying about making errors. For this reason, the drill begins with throws from the coach. Subsequently introducing batted balls to make the drill more gamelike adds a new dimension when players must field a ground ball and then make a feed.

The distance the ball is hit from the base dictates the type of feed. Balls fielded close to the bag, or when the fielders' momentum is going toward the bag, may be tossed underhand. Balls farther away may require the fielder to pivot before making the throw. Encourage players to restrict lower body movement, pivoting with the upper body mostly. Shortstops will find it easier to make the pivot on balls hit to their left if they place their right foot slightly forward when fielding the ball. For second-base players, their left foot should be slightly forward when fielding. Insist that fielders show the ball in their throwing hand without hiding it with the glove.

60. Coach's Choice Double Play

Purpose: To develop the double-play pivot by the shortstop and second-base player.

Number of Players: 7
Equipment: 1 baseball, 1 fungo bat
Time: 12 to 15 minutes

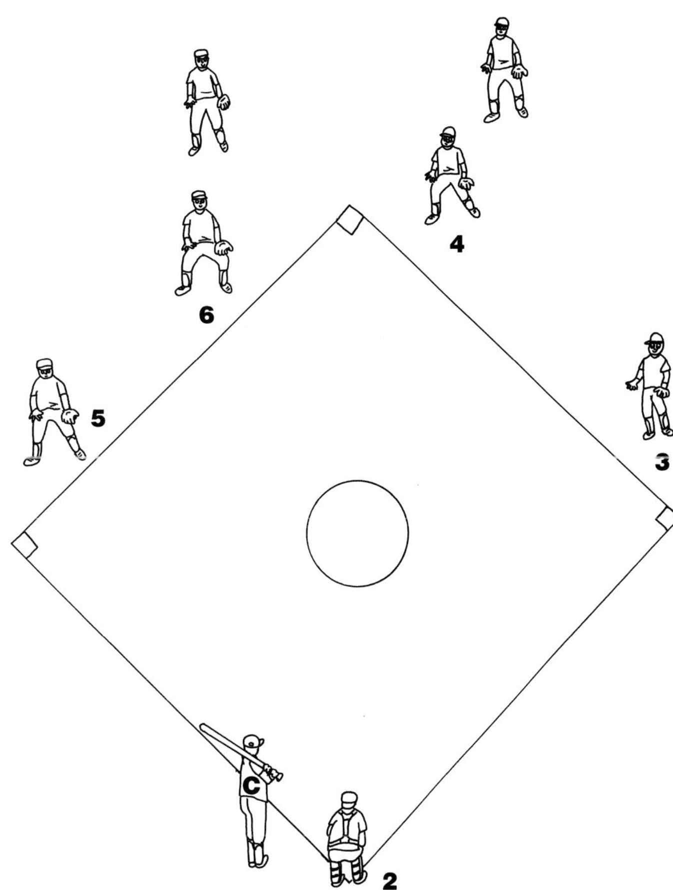

1. Position infielders at double-play depth. Station a second pair of middle infielders awaiting their turn behind the first pair.
2. Position a catcher at home plate to catch the ball returned by the first-base player.
3. A coach assumes a position at home plate with the catcher.
4. The coach hits the ball to any infielder he chooses.
5. The fielder to whom the ball is hit begins a double play by fielding the ball and throwing to second base.
6. The player receiving the ball at second base completes the double play by throwing to first.
7. The first-base player returns to ball to the catcher, who gives it to the coach.
8. Repeat.

This drill helps keep players focused. It is gamelike because the players aren't sure where the coach will be hitting the ball. Encourage players to communicate with one another before the ball is hit. For example, the third-base player might say to the second-base player, "If the ball is hit to me, I'm coming to you." This kind of communication helps reduce confusion when the ball is hit.

61. Second-Base Positioning 

Purpose: To develop the second-base player's understanding of how to modify positioning for the situation presented.

Number of Players: 1
Equipment: None
Time: 5 to 7 minutes

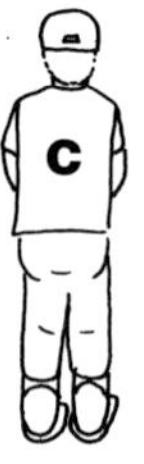

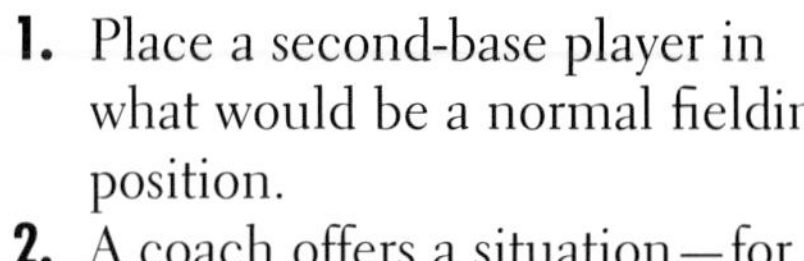

1. Place a second-base player in what would be a normal fielding position.

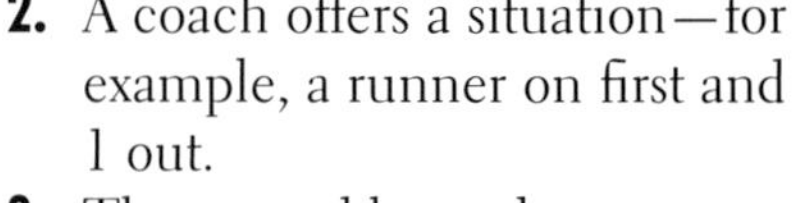

2. A coach offers a situation—for example, a runner on first and 1 out.

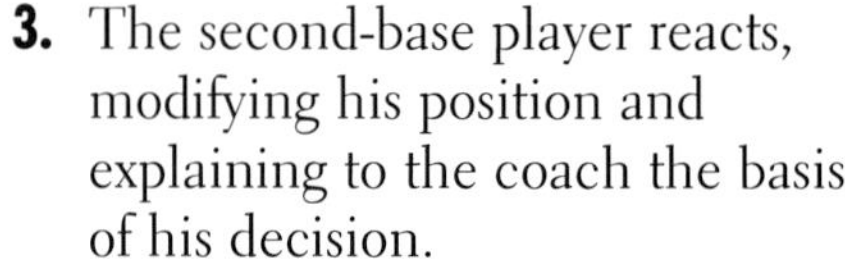

3. The second-base player reacts, modifying his position and explaining to the coach the basis of his decision.

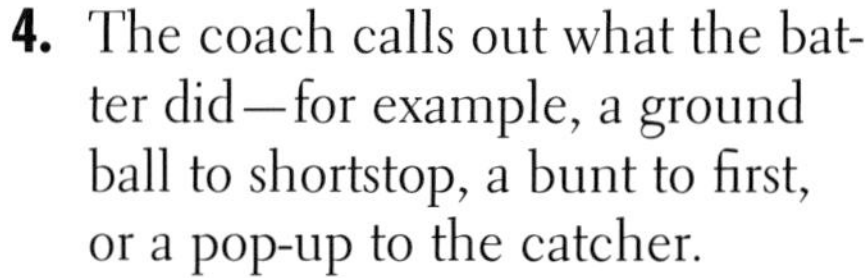

4. The coach calls out what the batter did—for example, a ground ball to shortstop, a bunt to first, or a pop-up to the catcher.
5. The second-base player moves to the position for which he is responsible—for example, covering or backing up first.
6. Repeat.

One-on-one sessions with coaches help determine how much players have learned. To see whether they have a clear understanding of the situation, ask players why they adjusted their positioning. This drill may be done in the outfield using two game markers as bases, and it can be used for all positions.

62. Second-Base Player Bunt 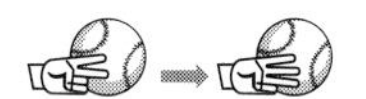

Purpose: To develop the second-base player's technique for covering first base on a bunt.

Number of Players: 5
Equipment: Catcher's equipment, 2 baseballs
Time: 10 to 12 minutes

1. Place a pitcher, catcher, first-base player, and second-base player in positions assuming an imaginary runner on first base and a potential bunt situation. Position another second-base player in the outfield grass awaiting his turn.
2. The pitcher throws the ball to the catcher.
3. A coach, standing at home plate, rolls a ball simulating a bunt to the pitcher, first-base player, or catcher.
4. The second-base player breaks to first base as fast as he can, giving the fielder an inside target to avoid hitting the imaginary runner.
5. Switch second-base players and repeat.

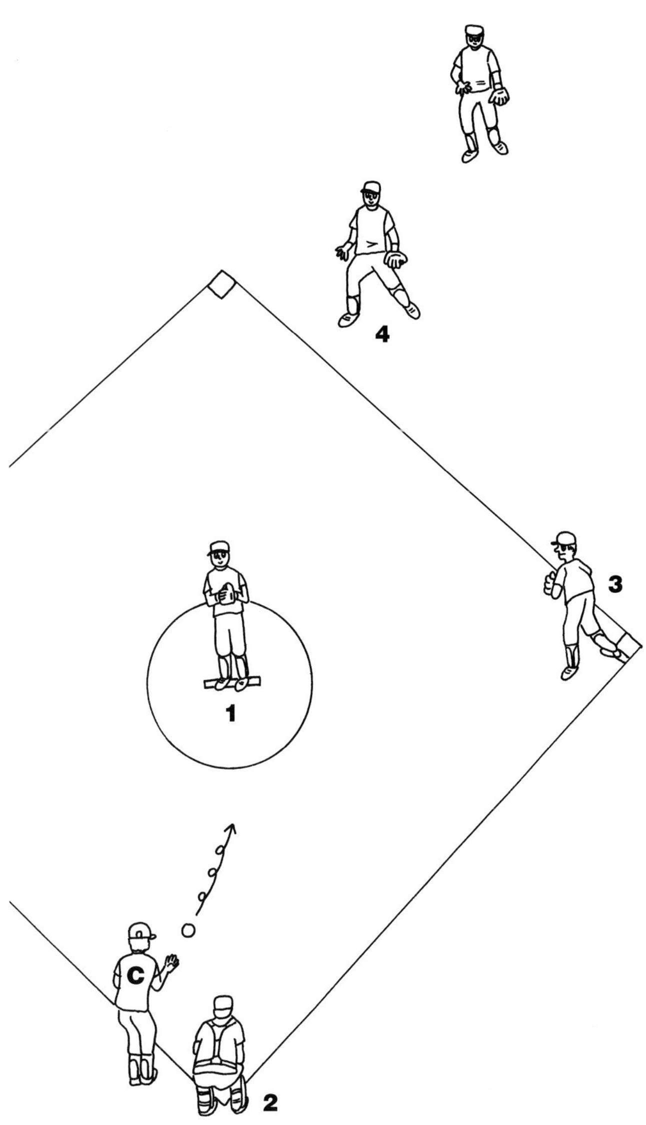

One of the most difficult plays in baseball is when second-base players have to cover first base on a bunt while there is a runner on first base. They must be able to get to second base if a ground ball is hit to the left side or to first base if a bunt is hit. Communication with teammates and getting to the base as fast as possible to be in balance to receive the throw help second-base player make this play. To make the drill more gamelike, add base runners.

63. Second-Base Player Steal Response 

Purpose: To develop the second-base player's technique for covering second base on a steal attempt.

Number of Players: 3
Equipment: Catcher's equipment, 1 baseball
Time: 8 to 10 minutes

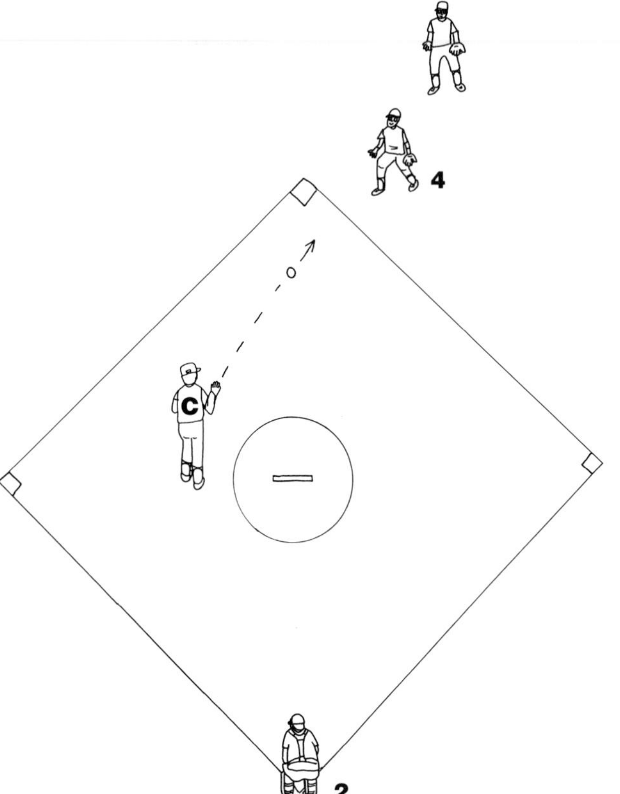

1. Position a second-base player in a fielding position that assumes a runner on first base. Position another second-base player in the outfield grass awaiting her turn.
2. Position a catcher at home plate.
3. When a coach positioned by the pitcher's mound raises his hand, the reserve infielder standing on the outside grass pretends she is one of the players on the bench and hollers, "Steal!"
4. The actual second-base player breaks for second base. The coach throws to the second-base player, who applies the tag to the imaginary runner.
5. The second-base player exchanges places with the reserve infielder.
6. After several repetitions, alternating second-base players, the coach moves to home plate.
7. The action is repeated but instead of throwing to second, the coach flips the ball to the catcher, who throws to second base.
8. Repeat, alternating second-base players.

With a runner at first, second-base players play a couple of steps closer to second base and toward home plate. They are generally responsible for covering second on a steal attempt with a right-handed hitter at the plate. They need to be in position to catch the ball before it arrives.

Some coaches like to teach players to straddle the base in this situation. I prefer that players have their left foot touching the inside portion of the base closest to home. This allows them to field low throws more efficiently. Whichever method you prefer, insist that second-base player have their glove above their waist so they can come down with the glove, catch the ball, and apply the tag in one motion. Don't allow them to extend their arms in front and bring the glove back to tag unless handling an errant throw.

64. Shortstop Bunt

Purpose: To develop the shortstop's technique for covering second base on a bunt.

Number of Players: 8
Equipment: Catcher's equipment, 1 baseball, 3 helmets
Time: 12 to 15 minutes

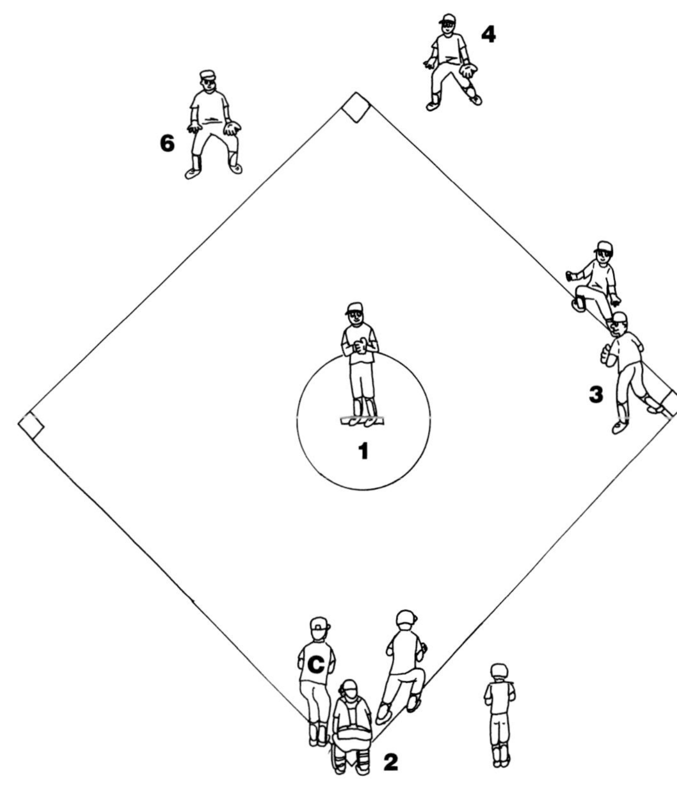

1. Place a first-base player, second-base player, and shortstop in the appropriate fielding positions for a possible bunt. Place a pitcher and catcher in their normal positions.
2. Position a runner at first base and another in the batter's box. Position a third base runner in the on-deck circle.
3. Position a coach beside the runner in the batter's box.
4. The pitcher comes to a set position. If the runner at first takes too much of a lead, the pitcher may throw to first.
5. The pitcher throws to the catcher.
6. As the ball crosses the plate, the coach rolls the ball, simulating a bunt. The runner on first goes to second, and the runner at home runs to first.
7. Whoever fields the ball tries to make the play at second base with the shortstop covering, if possible.
8. The last fielder with the ball returns it to the catcher.
9. Repeat.

Catchers usually call out to which base fielders should try to make the play. For this drill, catchers should call as many plays to second base as possible. Shortstops should be in position to catch the ball early, with their shoulders squared to the player who has the ball. This position should be slightly in front of the base. Unless a slow runner is at the plate, the chances of a double play are slim. The primary focus should be getting the out.

65. Shortstop Steal

Purpose: To develop the shortstop's technique for covering second base on a steal attempt while focusing on the hitter.

Number of Players: 3
Equipment: Catcher's equipment, 1 baseball, 1 fungo bat
Time: 8 to 10 minutes

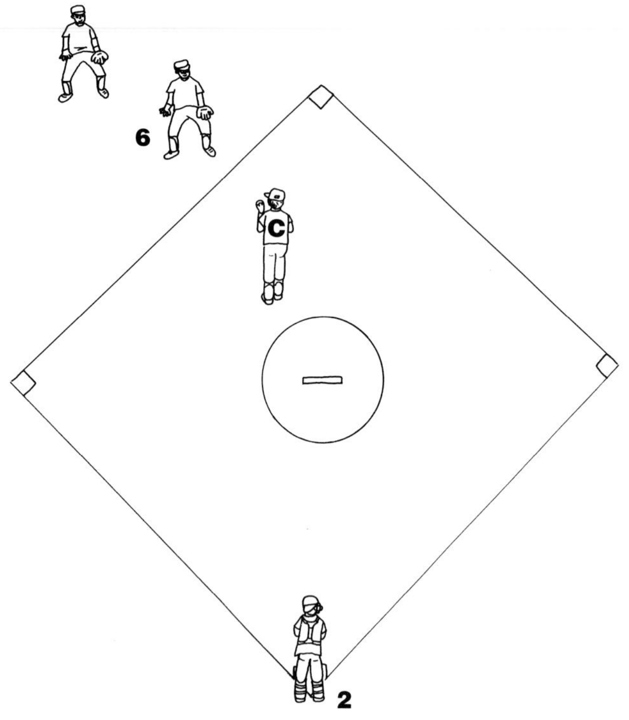

1. Position a shortstop in a fielding position that assumes a runner on first base. Position a reserve shortstop on the outfield grass awaiting his turn.
2. Position a catcher at home plate.
3. A coach, standing by the pitcher's mound, raises his hand.
4. The reserve infielder, pretending to be one of the players on the bench whose responsibility it is to watch the runners on base, hollers, "Steal!"
5. The shortstop moves to second base as quickly as possible. The coach throws the ball to the base for the shortstop to apply the tag on the imaginary runner.
6. After several repetitions by both shortstops, the coach moves to home plate. Instead of throwing the ball, he flips it to the catcher, who throws to second.
7. Occasionally, after the reserve player says "steal" and the shortstop begins to move, the coach hits a ground ball to the left of the shortstop.
8. Repeat, alternating shortstops.

Shortstops are generally responsible for covering second base when a left-handed hitter is at bat and a runner is on first base. This may change if the batter is known to hit consistently to the left side of the infield or if the pitcher is overpowering the hitter. Shortstops should move to the base quickly but watch the hitter and be able to recover to field a ball hit in their direction. Adding the coach to occasionally hit ground balls in this drill helps shortstops focus on the hitter. Shortstops should position themselves slightly in front of second base to receive the throw from the catcher. Holding the glove above the waist allows them to catch and come down in one motion to apply the tag on all balls thrown at or below waist level.

66. Shortstop Pivot 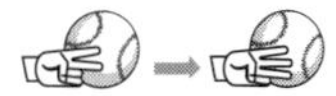

Purpose: To develop the shortstop's double-play pivot.

Number of Players: 3
Equipment: 1 baseball
Time: 8 to 10 minutes

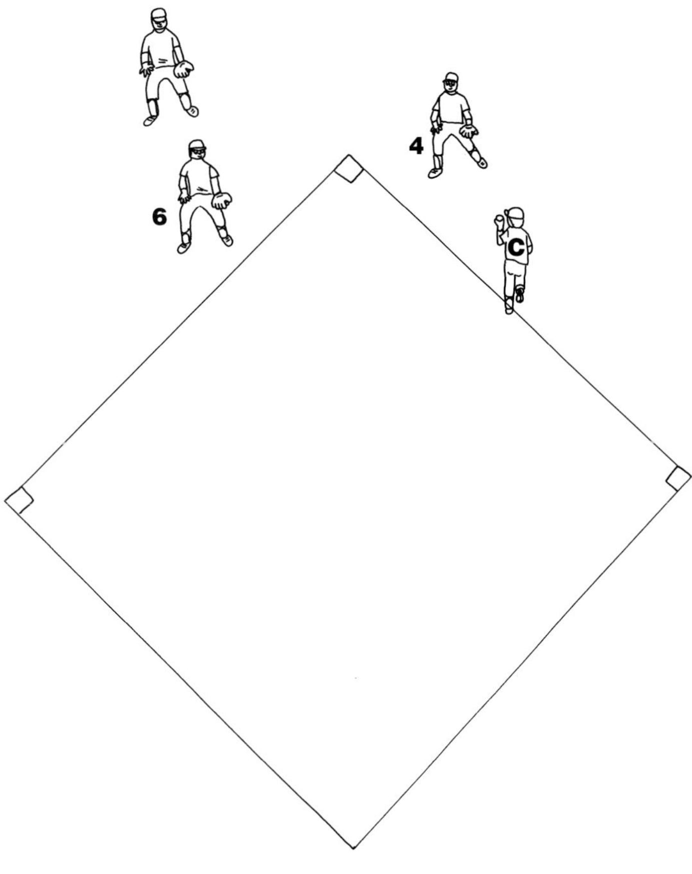

1. Position a shortstop and second-base player at double-play depth (a couple of steps closer to home and over toward second base). Position a second shortstop in the outfield grass awaiting her turn.
2. A coach, standing in the base path halfway between first and second base, throws a ball to the second-base player.
3. The second-base player throws to the shortstop, who has moved to cover second base.
4. The shortstop completes the play by throwing the ball to the coach.
5. Switch shortstops and repeat.

Since the focus of this drill is the shortstop's pivot, throw balls to the second-base player instead of hitting them. This allows the second-base player to feed the shortstop on each play and eliminates the possibility of errors when fielding ground balls. When turning the double play, the shortstop should move to second base to be in position early and should square her shoulders to her target (the second-base player). The shortstop's right foot should be in contact with the base. If she has no pressure from the base runner, she catches the ball, pushes off with her right foot, and makes the throw. If the runner is creating pressure, she shuffles her feet toward right field using a step-together-step motion to clear herself from the runner's path.

67. Shortstop Pickoff 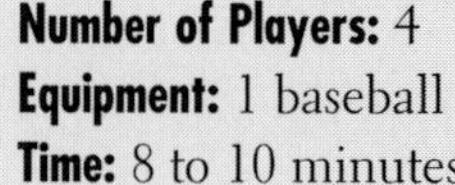

Purpose: To develop the shortstop's pickoff technique.

Number of Players: 4
Equipment: 1 baseball
Time: 8 to 10 minutes

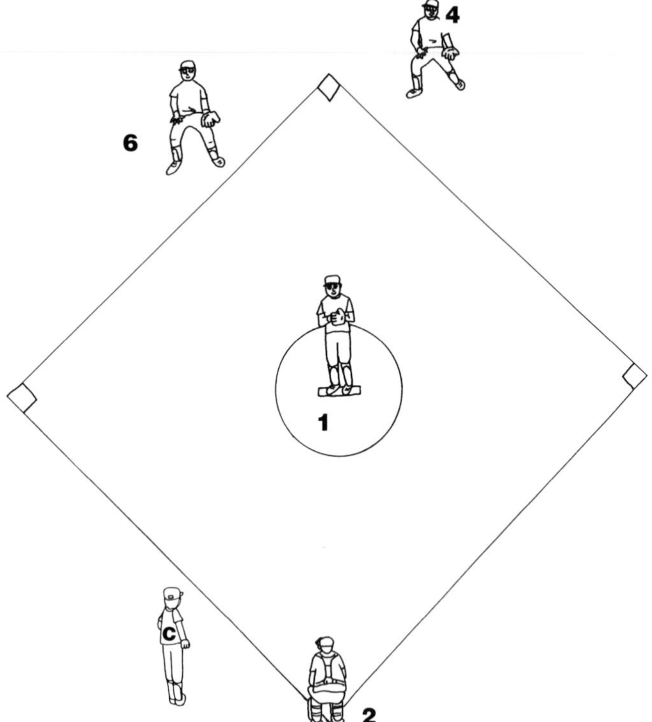

1. Place a shortstop, second-base player, pitcher, and catcher in their fielding positions.
2. An imaginary runner is at second base.
3. A coach gives a verbal signal that the pickoff attempt is on.
4. The second-base player moves toward second base, then quickly away.
5. As the second-base player begins to move away, the shortstop moves quickly to second base.
6. The catcher gives a target, then lowers his glove as a signal for the pitcher to turn and throw.
7. The pitcher throws to the target given by the catcher.
8. Repeat several times

The key to this play is timing. The pitcher must turn and throw as the shortstop is approaching the base. To help eliminate the confusion of not knowing the play is on, the catcher gives the pitcher a target by holding his glove up but gives no signal as to what kind of pitch he wants. If one or both of the middle infielders don't know the play is on and aren't moving, the catcher continues to hold his glove as a target without dropping it. In this case, the pitcher steps back off the rubber and the play is off. After running the drill as described above, add base runners and a third-base player. Tell the runners that if the pitcher throws to the plate they must steal third base. This encourages base runners to take a large lead, increasing their chances of getting picked off.

68. Third-Base Player Bunt 

Purpose: To develop the third-base player's technique for fielding bunts.

Number of Players: 4
Equipment: 1 baseball, 1 fungo bat
Time: 8 to 10 minutes

1. Position a third-base player even with the infield grass, with a reserve third-base player behind him awaiting his turn.
2. Place a first-base player and a catcher at their defensive positions.
3. A coach, standing at home plate, lowers his fungo bat as if to bunt.
4. This lowering of the bat signals the third-base player to charge home plate.
5. After lowering his bat, the coach rolls a ball to simulate a bunt.
6. The third-base player fields the ball and throws it to first.
7. The first-base player returns the ball to the catcher.
8. Switch third-base players and repeat.

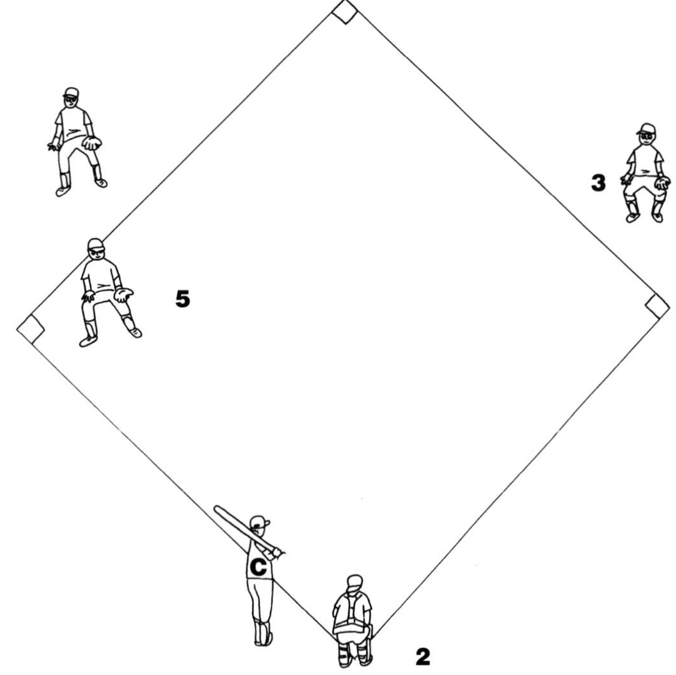

The third-base player's position for playing the bunt is dictated by the number of runners on base, the hitter's speed, the batter's ball and strike count, the score, and so forth. When fielding the bunt, third-base player charges quickly, plant his dominant foot next to the ball, picks up the ball, steps, and throws to first. Older players should practice barehanded pickups for faster execution because they won't always have time to straighten up to throw. Encourage them to pick the ball up and deliver it using a sidearm motion.

69. Third-Base Player Double Play 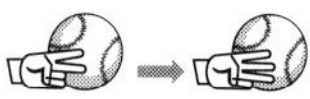

Purpose: To develop the third-base player's double-play decision-making skills.

Number of Players: 5
Equipment: 1 baseball, 1 fungo bat
Time: 8 to 10 minutes

1. Position a third-base player at double-play depth (a step or two behind third base depending on the speed of the runner). Locate a second third-base player behind third base awaiting his turn.
2. Position a second-base player, first-base player, and catcher in their fielding positions.
3. Imaginary runners are on first and second base.
4. A coach, standing at home plate, hits a ground ball to the third-base player, who decides whether to touch third and throw to first or to throw to second to begin the double play.
5. Repeat, alternating third-base players.

Where the third-base player decides to begin the double play will be dictated by the location of the hit ball. If the ball is to the third-base player's left side, he should play the ball to second base since his momentum is already going that way. If the ball is hit at him or to his backhand side, he should touch third base, then throw to first. If he has to charge the slow roller, he may decide first base is his only play. After executing the drill as described above, add base runners at home plate and first and second base.

70. Outfield Body-in-Motion Technique 

Purpose: To develop the outfielder's body-in-motion defensive technique.

Number of Players: 5
Equipment: 2 baseballs, 1 fungo bat
Time: 12 to 15 minutes

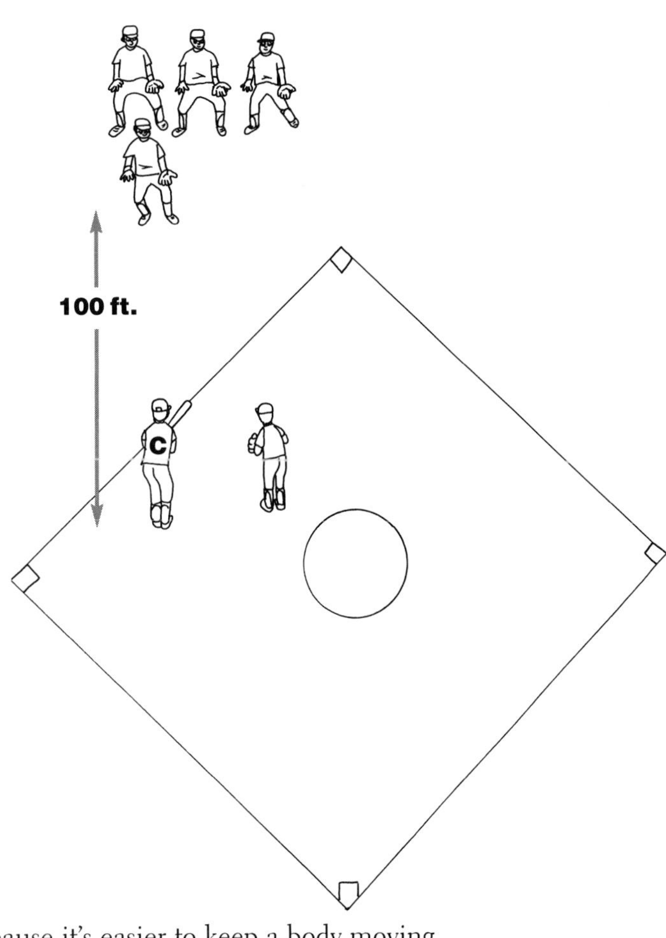

1. Position four outfielders in a line about 100 feet from a coach, who will be hitting a variety of ground balls, line drives, and fly balls with a fungo bat.
2. Position a fifth player next to the coach to simulate a cut-off player and receive throws from the outfielders.
3. On the coach's signal, the first outfielder in line slowly moves toward the coach.
4. The coach hits the ball. The outfielder reacts to the ball, fields it, steps forward with the dominant foot, and throws to the player standing next to the coach. During the throwing motion, players should use the dominant foot to push off with while stepping with the nondominant foot.
5. Repeat with all of the outfielders.

Players should experiment with a variety of techniques for getting a good jump on the ball. Some players prefer the body-in-motion method because it's easier to keep a body moving that is already moving than to begin moving a body from a stationary position. Outfielders' motion should be in small steps toward the hitter, much like that of an infielder. They should have their legs slightly flexed to accelerate pushing off in either direction.

71. Outfield Straight-Up Technique 

Purpose: To develop the outfielder's straight-up defensive technique.

Number of Players: 5
Equipment: 1 tennis ball, 1 tennis racket
Time: 12 to 15 minutes

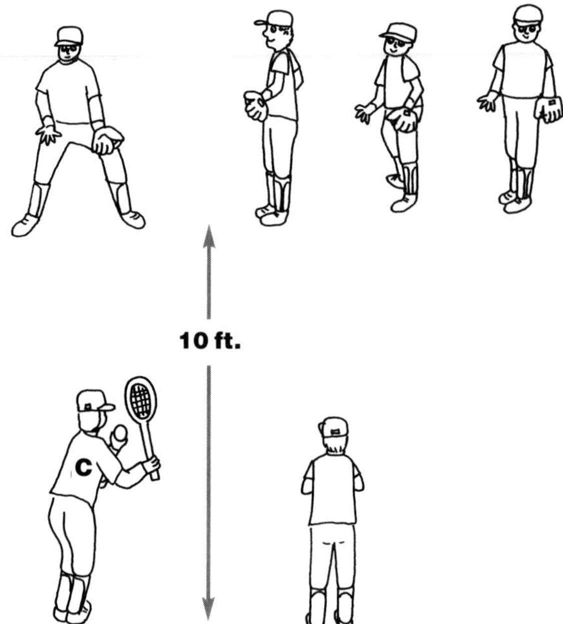

1. Position four outfielders in a line in the outfield.
2. Place a fifth player next to the coach, who is stationed 10 feet from the players.
3. On the coach's signal, the first outfielder steps up and assumes a straight-up defensive position.
4. The coach strikes a tennis ball into the air.
5. The outfielder reacts to the flight of the ball, fields it, tosses it to the next outfielder in line, and jogs to the end of the line.
6. The next outfielder, now at the front of the line, tosses the ball to the player standing beside the coach.
7. Repeat with each outfielder.

Players love the variety a tennis racket and tennis balls bring to practice. Coaches generally can strike tennis balls more accurately with greater height, which makes tracking the balls more challenging. Some outfielders prefer the straight-up stance, which is executed by having the toes facing the hitter, shoulders square, legs slightly flexed, with weight slightly forward on the balls of the feet. This position allows them to move either to their glove side by pushing off with their dominant foot or performing a crossover step, or to their throwing side by pushing off with their now-dominant foot or performing a crossover step. The most difficult balls to field are the ones hit directly behind players in the straight-up stance. To get to these balls, players should drop their dominant foot in a backward motion, look for the ball, hustle to the area of the ball, and field it.

72. Outfield Angled-Body Technique

Purpose: To develop the outfielder's angled-body defensive technique.

Number of Players: 5
Equipment: 5 baseballs
Time: 12 to 15 minutes

1. Position five outfielders, each with a baseball, in a line on the outfield grass.
2. Station a coach 20 feet from the line of players.
3. The first outfielder steps away from the other players, throws the coach his ball, and assumes an angled-body position.
4. The coach throws the ball in the air to the right or left of, or directly behind, the player.
5. The player reacts to the throw, hustles to the ball, and makes the catch.
6. The player moves to the end of the line.
7. Repeat several times with each outfielder.

Some players prefer the angled-body position when playing outfield. The angled-body position is executed by placing one foot in front of the other, assuming a sideways stance to the hitter. Which foot is forward is dictated by the hitter's tendencies, the amount of space to be covered on either side of the outfielder, and player preference. Encourage outfielders to look for the direction of the ball, hustle in that direction, and then look for the ball. Running the entire way while looking at the ball, particularly balls directly behind them, affects speed. Playing an angled stance allows outfielders to get a good jump on balls hit in the direction their chest is facing and on balls hit both in front of and behind them. Balls hit in the direction that their back is facing may be a bit more difficult. To field these balls, they must pivot on their back foot while using a swing step with their front foot.

73. Outfield Ground Ball

Purpose: To develop the outfielder's technique for fielding ground balls.

Number of Players: 7
Equipment: 1 baseball, 1 fungo bat
Time: 12 to 15 minutes

1. Position four players in a line in the outfield.
2. Station a fifth player next to the coach at the pitcher's mound.
3. Place second- and third-base players in their defensive positions.
4. The first outfielder in line steps up and assumes a ready position.
5. The coach hits a ground ball to the outfielder.
6. The outfielder fields the ball and tosses it to one of the outfielders still in line, who throws it to the player beside the coach.
7. Repeat, rotating outfielders.
8. After several rotations, add imaginary base runners at home and/or first base.
9. When the coach hits the ground ball, the outfielder charges the ball and throws to the base that the coach calls out (second or third base).
10. Repeat, rotating outfielders.

Outfielders' technique in fielding ground balls depends on such factors as the batter's speed, the number of runners on base, the game situation (inning and score), and field conditions. When outfielders aren't in a hurry to make a throw, they can hustle to the ball, field it in front of them like infielders do, and throw to a base. When they must get the ball to a base in a hurry, they hustle to the ball, continue to charge it while playing it off their glove side, step, and throw. Encourage outfielders to use an overhand throw to the bases.

74. Outfield Communication 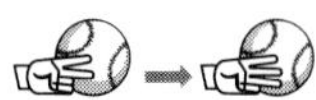

Purpose: To develop outfield communication.

Number of Players: 4
Equipment: 2 baseballs, 1 fungo bat
Time: 8 to 10 minutes

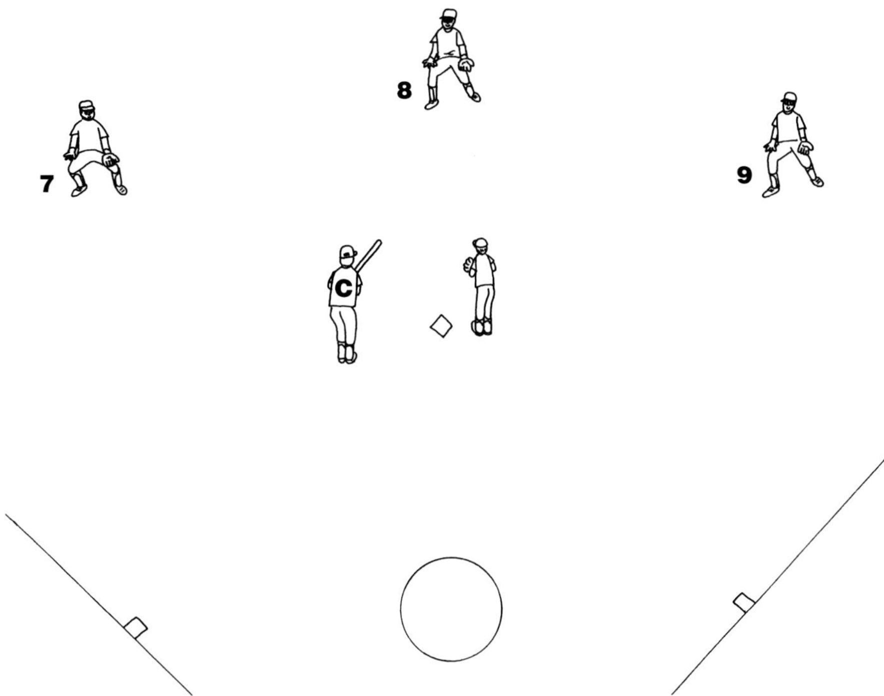

1. Position one player each in center, right, and left field. Station a fourth player next to the coach at second base to receive outfielders' throws.
2. The coach hits a fly ball to one of the gaps between the outfielders.
3. Outfielders communicate with one another as to who will make the play.
4. The outfielder making the play throws the ball to the player at second base.
5. Repeat.

The center fielder runs the show. It is his responsibility to call off the other outfielders if he feels he can make the play on all balls that are between the outfielders. If both the center fielder and another player call for the ball, the center fielder's job is to call off the other player and the other players' job is to yield to the center fielder. Discourage center fielders from going into another outfielder's territory just to make a play. This sort of behavior damages a team's spirit. Instruct outfielders to call out loudly "I've got it" when calling for the ball.

75. Infield–Outfield Communication 

Purpose: To improve infield–outfield communication.

Number of Players: 8
Equipment: 2 baseballs, 1 fungo bat
Time: 12 to 15 minutes

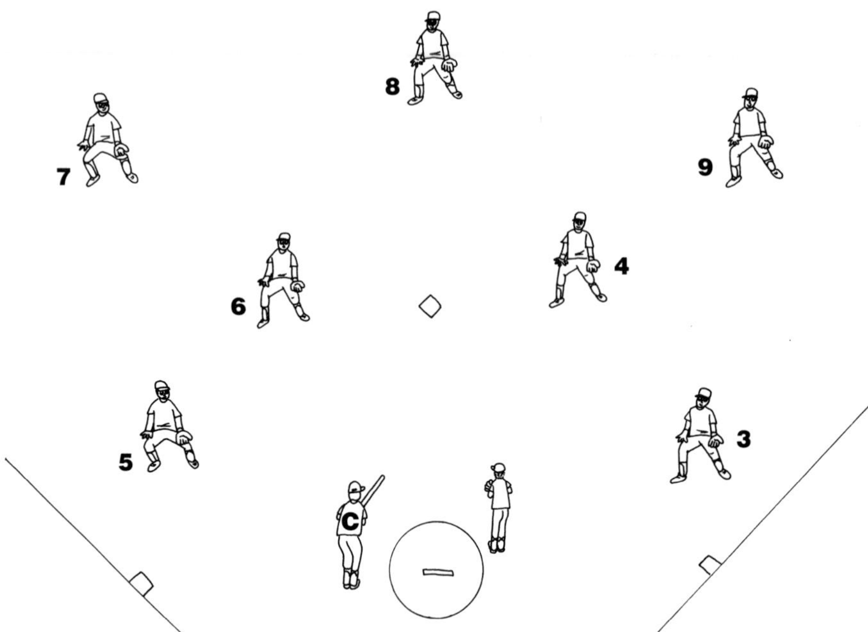

1. Station players so that all infield and outfield positions except pitcher and catcher are occupied.
2. Position another player next to the coach, who is standing at the pitcher's mound.
3. The coach hits a fly ball between the infielders and the outfielders.
4. Players communicate with one another while making the play.
5. The player fielding the ball returns it to the player beside the coach.
6. Repeat.

Standing at the pitcher's mound rather than home plate allows the coach more control of the balls he's hitting. Before starting the drill, instruct the players in the chain of command that should be used in the communication process between infielders and outfielders. The center fielder calls off the right and left fielders, the outfielders call off the infielders, and the shortstop and second base-base player call off the first and third-base players. The infielders should go as hard as they can for the fly balls until they hear the outfielders call them off. If an outfielder doesn't call for a ball, it means he can't get to it.

76. Outfield Throwing 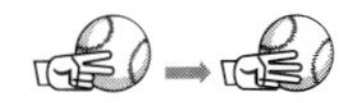

Purpose: To improve the outfielder's throwing accuracy.

Number of Players: 4
Equipment: 1 baseball, 4 game markers
Time: 8 to 10 minutes

1. Form a square with four game markers and position a player at each corner—75 feet apart for intermediate players and 100 feet for advanced players. One player has a ball.
2. The player with the ball throws overhand to the player to her right.
3. The player catching the ball throws the ball to the player diagonally across the square.
4. Repeat the pattern of throwing to the right, then across for several minutes.
5. Reverse the pattern by throwing to the player on the left, then across the square.
6. Repeat.

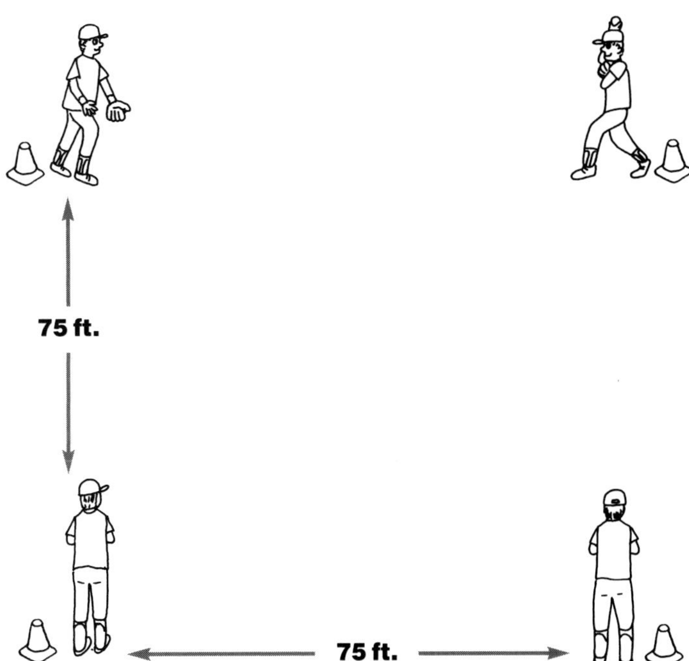

As player accuracy begins to improve, increase the distance between the players. To help prevent the ball from curving, encourage players to throw overhand instead of sidearm or three-quarter style. Instruct players to catch, step, and throw. The catch-step-throw procedure helps ensure a faster release of the ball than if players took several steps before throwing.

77. Outfield Relay 

Purpose: To improve the outfielder's throwing accuracy and speed when releasing the ball.

Number of Players: 6
Equipment: 2 baseballs
Time: 8 to 10 minutes

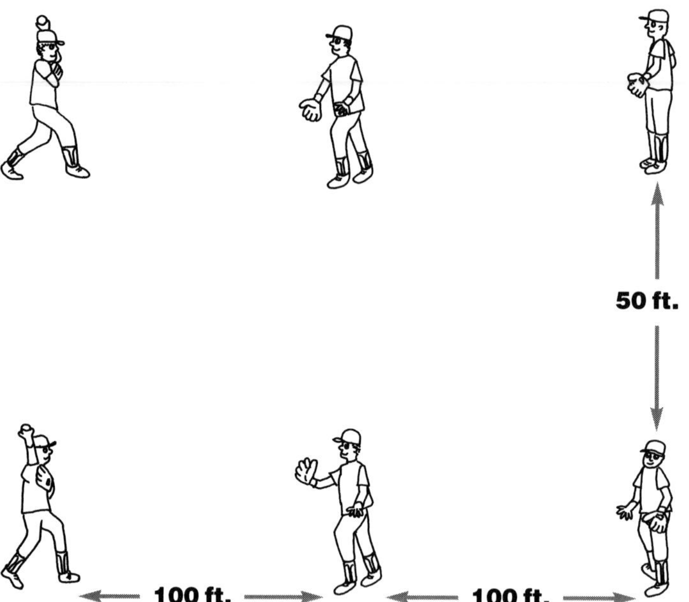

1. Divide players into two teams of three players. One player on each team has a ball.
2. Position the teams in two straight lines 50 feet apart, with the players in each line spaced 100 feet apart.
3. On a coach's signal, the player with the ball throws it to the player on his team who is standing in the middle.
4. The middle player throws the ball to the last player on his team.
5. The last player in line throws the ball back to the middle player, who throws it to the first player, who started the action.
6. The players change roles. The first player in line moves to the middle, the middle player moves to the end, and the end player moves to the front of the line.
7. Repeat the throwing pattern in steps 3 to 5.

Discourage outfielders from making sidearm throws, which tend to curve. Players standing in the middle should play sideways to allow for a faster release to the next player instead of having their back turned to the next player. Encourage players to take as few steps as possible when holding the ball before throwing to the next player. Encourage the catch-step-throw technique.

78. Outfielder Net Game 

Purpose: To develop the outfielder's throwing accuracy and speed.

Number of Players: 8
Equipment: 12 baseballs, 8 game markers, 1 safety net
Time: 10 to 12 minutes

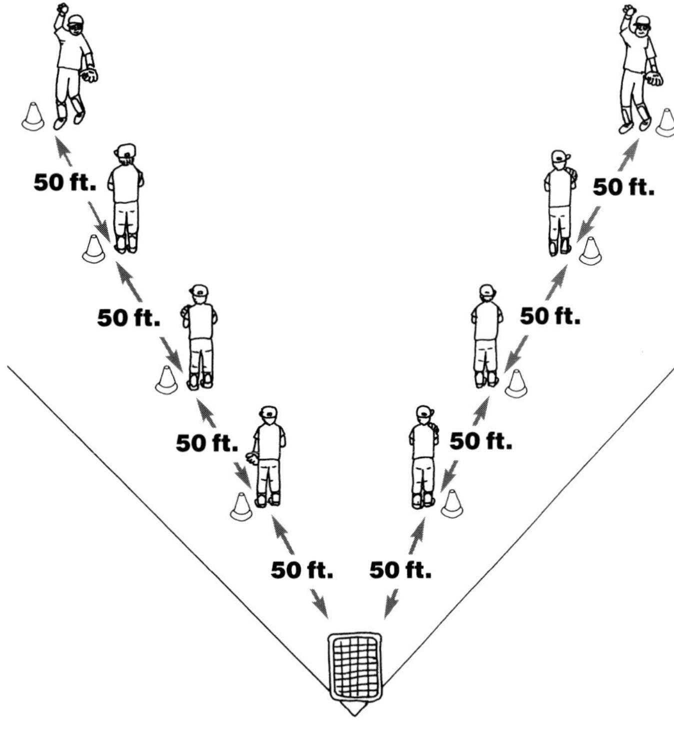

1. Position a safety net at home plate.
2. Use eight game markers to designate two lines extending 200 feet into the outfield from home plate. Space the markers 50 feet apart within each line, beginning with the first marker 50 feet from home plate.
3. Divide eight players into two teams of four. Position one player by each game marker. Place six baseballs next to the player on each team who is farthest from home plate.
4. On a coach's signal, the player farthest from home plate throws a ball to the next player in line.
5. The players toss the ball down the line until it reaches the last player, who then throws the ball in the safety net.
6. If the last player misses the net, the first person picks up another ball and repeats the action.
7. If the last player hits the net, he sprints to the first player's position, picks up a ball, and repeats the action.
8. When each player has had a chance to assume each position and has returned to his original position, the team is finished.
9. The first team finished wins.

Encourage players to use overhand throws for accuracy. Relay players receiving the ball should stand sideways to help release the ball faster. Players throwing the ball to relay players should throw the ball to the relay players' glove side. To add variety, add more players or change the distance between players.

79. Outfielding in the Sun 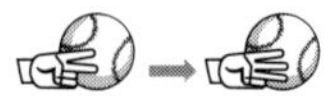

Purpose: To develop technique for catching fly balls on a sunny day.

Number of Players: 3
Equipment: 1 tennis ball, 1 tennis racket
Time: 8 to 10 minutes

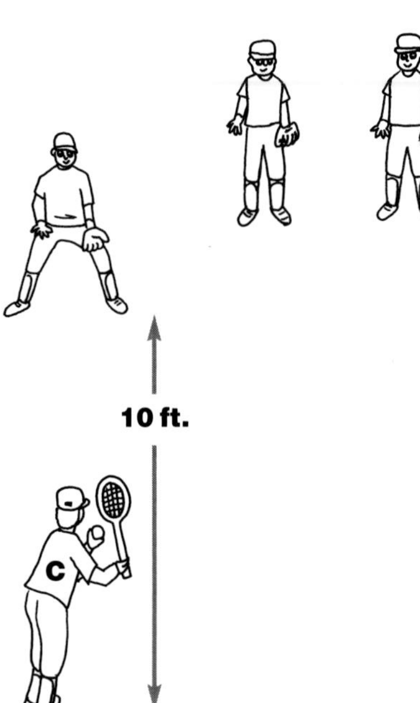

1. Position players in the outfield next to one another.
2. Station a coach 10 feet from the players with a tennis racket and tennis balls.
3. The first player steps up and assumes a ready position.
4. The coach strikes the tennis ball as high as he can toward the sun.
5. The fielder blocks the sun, catches the ball, and returns it to the coach.
6. Repeat, rotating fielders.

Encourage players to use their bare hand to block the sun when fielding the ball. Turning their body so they aren't facing the sun also helps. Using tennis balls reduces the chance of injuries.

80. Fielding Near an Outfield Fence

Purpose: To develop the outfielder's technique for playing balls near the outfield fence.

Number of Players: 5
Equipment: 1 baseball, 1 fungo bat
Time: 10 to 12 minutes

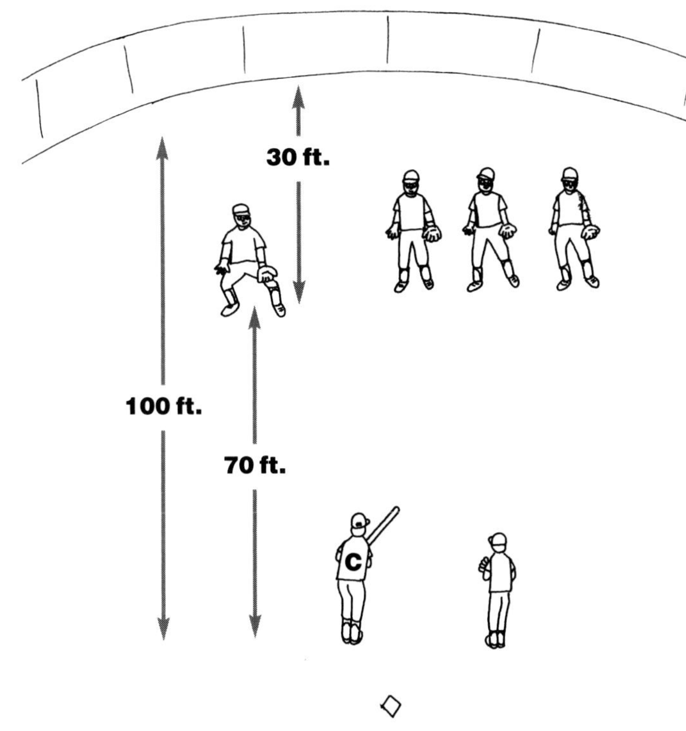

1. Position four outfielders in a line 30 feet inside the outfield fence.
2. Station another player and a coach 100 feet from the outfield fence, 70 feet from the line of outfielders.
3. The first outfielder in line steps up and assumes a ready position. The next player in line communicates how much room the player fielding the ball has to make the play.
4. The coach hits a fly ball behind the outfielder.
5. The outfielder turns, hustles back to the fence, touches the fence, looks for the ball, and then makes the play. At the same time, the next player in line is constantly communicating to the fielder how much room he has to make the play.
6. The outfielder throws the ball to the player standing beside the coach.
7. Repeat, rotating outfielders.

Fields with fences present a safety problem for players if the players haven't practiced fielding technique on how to use the fence. To avoid having players collide with the fence, instruct them to run to the fence and touch it, if time permits, before catching the ball. It's safer for outfielders to run to the fence and find the ball than it is for them to watch the ball the whole way and collide with the fence. Having other outfielders communicating the distance to the fence and the location of the ball also helps prevent injuries.

Of course, not all fields have fences. This drill can be practiced using game markers as a temporary fence so that players can learn this technique and be ready to play on the fields that do have fences.

CHAPTER 6

Hitting Drills

Hitting a baseball is a very difficult action. If it weren't, getting a hit only 3 out of every 10 times at bat wouldn't be such a big deal. The .300 hitter is admired even though he fails 7 out of 10 times.

I believe hitting technique is an individual matter, with hitters feeling a little more comfortable when they do this or do that. I also believe that individual hitting style is the result of countless repetitions, adjustments, successes, and failures with the bat.

Although there are differences in the way players grip the bat, the way they put their body in motion for the swing, and the swing pattern itself, certain consistencies also need to be presented—starting with beginning players and then reviewed and reinforced with intermediate and advanced players.

The drills in this chapter can be used to improve players' ability to strike the ball by creating a better understanding of hand placement, head and foot position, and the concept of transfer of weight. I have also included activities to improve eye-hand coordination, to correct such common flaws as bailing out and hitching, and to help players gain a better understanding of the strike zone.

To address safety issues when hitting, this chapter also includes drills to help batters avoid getting hit by pitchers and to prevent the throwing of bats during the swing process. To ensure a safe environment, use modified equipment, such as safety bats and safety balls. Above all, create a safe environment for practicing hitting skills. Using safety balls for beginners is a must, as is the use of helmets for players at all levels. When using the hitting drills for station work, be sure to space the group properly and to hit in opposite directions so that it becomes impossible for a player in another group to be struck by a hit ball. Caution players awaiting a turn at bat to position themselves so they won't be hit with a foul ball or a bat thrown by a teammate. Create safety zones in which players are permitted to take practice swings.

Many of these drills can be used in station work or batting practice. Using small-group activities provides numerous repetitions for each player. During game situations, institute a no-walk rule so that beginning and intermediate players will have more opportunities for hitting. Vary the equipment used for station work to include batting tees, fat bats, and various types of balls.

Give players experiences in striking balls that they throw to themselves, that they hit stationary from a tee, and that are thrown by a pitcher. For players struggling to make contact, include opportunities to improve their swing pattern by using a stationary ball on a batting tee combined with such other activities as hitting with a pitcher throwing baseballs, a small group striking whiffle balls in a corner of the outfield, or players striking balls thrown by a coach kneeling behind the backstop. Using batting tees will allow struggling players to make contact and feel successful during practice. If players continue to struggle even with the batting tee, use a larger bat, such as a whiffle fat bat, or a larger ball, such as a softball-size whiffle ball. Observe and correct the most obvious flaws in players' swing pattern, starting with making sure their eyes watch the ball.

81. Turn Away

Purpose: To develop the batter's technique for avoiding being hit with a pitched ball.

Number of Players: 4
Equipment: 1 fleece ball, 4 helmets, 4 bats
Time: 5 to 7 minutes

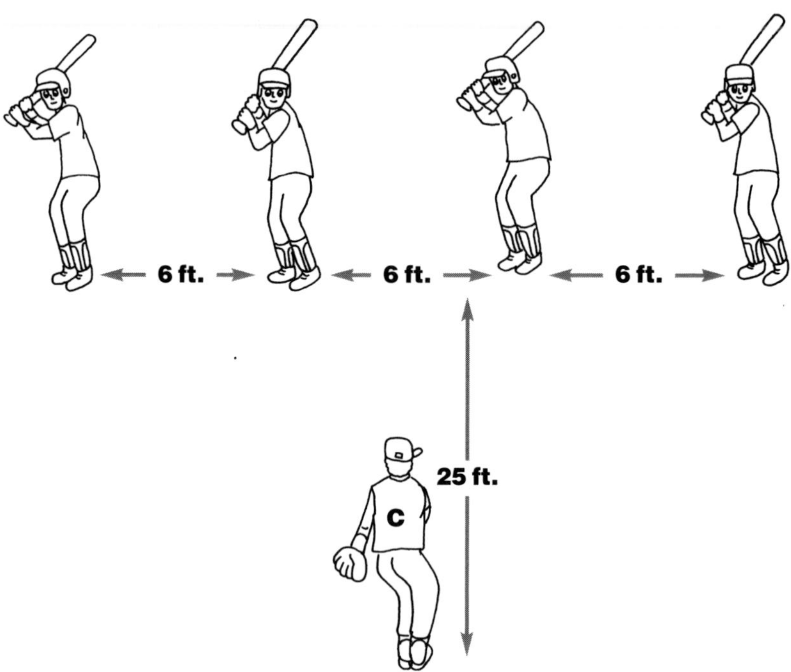

1. Position players in a line 6 feet apart. Each player holds a bat.
2. Players assume a batting stance.
3. A coach, standing about 25 feet from the players, winds up and makes a pretend pitch.
4. Players react to protect themselves from being hit with a pitched ball by turning down and away with their front shoulder.
5. Repeat.

Teach players the correct way to protect themselves: turning down and away from the ball. Turning the front shoulder down and away in a pivoting motion protects players from being hit in the face and chest with the ball. This drill provides numerous opportunities to practice this technique.

82. Avoiding Being Hit by a Pitch

Purpose: To develop the batter's technique for avoiding being hit by a pitched ball.

Number of Players: 4
Equipment: 5 fleece balls, 4 helmets, 1 bat
Time: 8 to 10 minutes

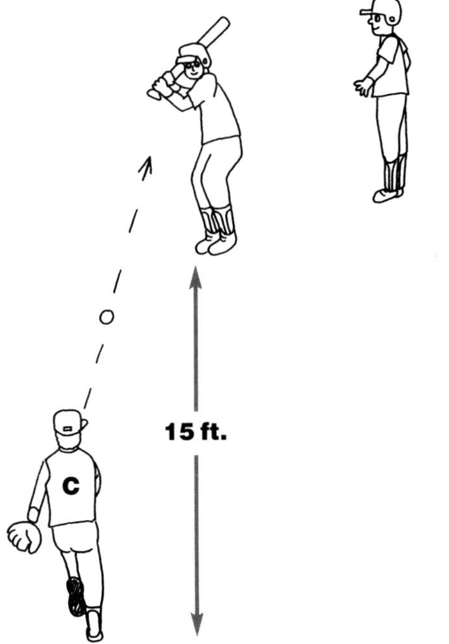

1. Position one player in a batting stance. Position the other players in a line behind the first batter awaiting their turn.
2. A coach, standing 15 feet from the batter, softly throws a fleece ball right at the batter's head.
3. As the ball comes toward the batter's head, the batter reacts by turning his front shoulder down and away in a pivoting action.
4. Repeat using all five fleece balls.
5. Rotate batters and begin again.

This is a safe way to reduce players' fear of getting struck with the ball. If they make a mistake by not reacting to the pitch during this drill, they won't be injured by a fleece ball. Initially, players may react slowly or even freeze when they see the ball coming at their head. Through repetition, they develop the technique of twisting down and away, which could prevent serious injury later in their careers. This drill should be a part of every beginning player's practice.

Note key to symbols, page 21

83. Plate Position

Purpose: To develop the batter's concept of the proper distance to stand from home plate.

Number of Players: 4
Equipment: 3 safety balls, 1 helmet, 1 bat, 1 batting tee
Time: 12 to 15 minutes

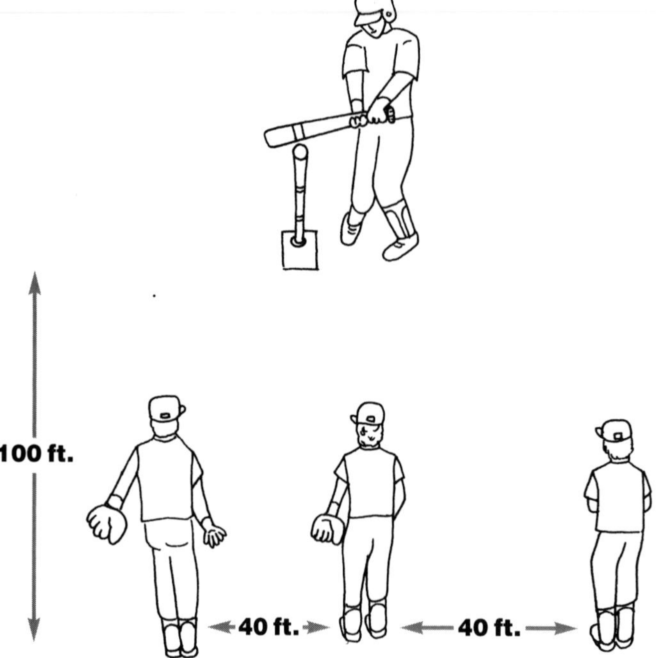

1. Position a batter standing next to the batting tee.
2. Position three fielders 40 feet apart and 100 feet from the batting tee to retrieve batted balls.
3. The hitter places a ball on the batting tee.
4. Next, the hitter extends his arms so that the portion of the bat with a piece of tape wrapped around it (the sweet spot) is touching the ball. The hitter should adjust the position of his feet accordingly.
5. The hitter strikes the ball off the tee, concentrating on having the taped part of the bat make contact.
6. Repeat until all balls have been hit.
7. Rotate players and begin again.

Placing a piece of tape around the sweet spot of the bat (where the trademark is located) gives players a visual cue as to where they want to strike the ball. Beginning players also need to know how far to stand from the plate. This exercise helps them position their feet a suitable distance from home plate. This distance varies according to the player's size and arm length and the length of the bat.

84. Band-Aid Grip

Purpose: To develop proper hand placement on the bat.

Number of Players: 4
Equipment: 16 safety balls, 4 helmets, 4 bats, 4 batting tees, 4 Band-Aids
Time: 5 to 7 minutes

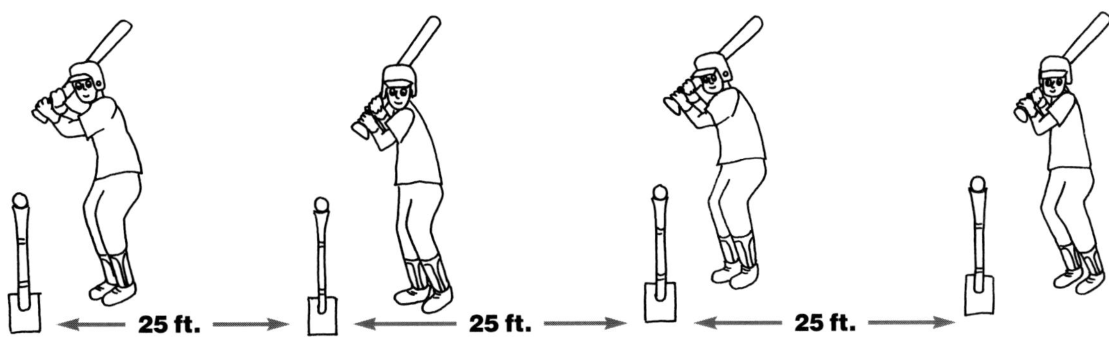

1. Position four batting tees 25 feet apart. Place one safety ball on each tee and three more beside each tee.
2. A coach places a Band-Aid on the base of the thumb of the left hand for right-handed batters (thumb of right hand for left-handed batters).
3. Batters assume a hitting position by the batting tees.
4. The coach calls out, "Squeeze the Band-Aid!"
5. Batters slide their top hand (right hand for right-handed batters, left hand for left-handed batters) down, contacting the bottom hand with the Band-Aid, squeeze so that they feel the Band-Aid with the top hand, and swing.
6. Players place another ball on the tee, await the coach's signal, and repeat the action.

Many beginning players separate their hands when gripping the bat. This drill gives them a visual cue to help remind them of proper hand placement.

85. Dropping the Bat

Purpose: To help prevent injury from hitters throwing bats.

Number of Players: 4
Equipment: 16 safety balls, 4 helmets, 4 bats, 4 batting tees, 4 game spots
Time: 5 to 7 minutes

1. Position four batting tees 25 feet apart.
2. Position a hitter at each batting tee.
3. Place a game spot to the left side and slightly in back of each hitter.
4. On a coach's command, batters swing, strike the ball, and drop the bat on the game spot.

Use this drill very early during the season to help prevent injury. Positioning the batting tees 25 feet apart helps prevent injury if a player throws the bat during the swing because he hasn't grasped the concept of swing and drop. Placing a game spot on the ground gives batters a visual cue of where to drop the bat.

86. Stationary Target

Purpose: To develop eye-hand coordination for striking.

Number of Players: 1
Equipment: 1 helmet, 1 bat, 1 Hit-N-Stik
Time: 3 to 5 minutes

1. Position a coach holding a Hit-N-Stik behind the backstop.
2. Position a batter in a good hitting position next to the Hit-N-Stik.
3. On the coach's signal, the batter swings the bat, trying to strike the ball at the end of the Hit-N-Stik.
4. Repeat, varying the level of the Hit-N-Stik as well as moving it inside and outside.

This drill offers a terrific one-on-one opportunity with the coach to correct any flaws in hitting mechanics. Players having trouble making contact benefit from this exercise. For these players, hold the Hit-N-Stik still. As players progress, add movement to the Hit-N-Stik.

87. Fat Bat

Purpose: To develop eye-hand coordination for striking.

Number of Players: 3
Equipment: 6 whiffle balls, 1 helmet, 1 fat bat, 1 batting tee
Time: 12 to 15 minutes

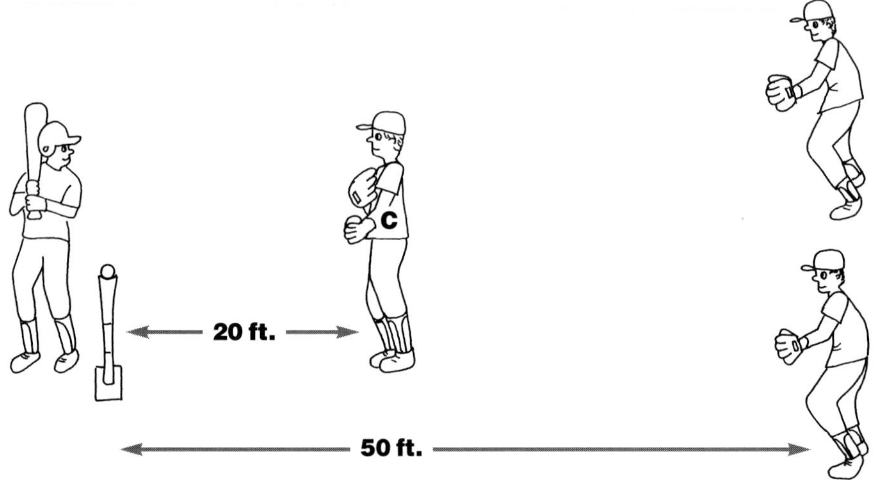

1. Position two fielders in a portion of the outfield 50 feet from the batting tee.
2. Position a batter next to the batting tee.
3. On the coach's signal, the batter strikes the ball off the batting tee using a fat bat (an oversize whiffle ball bat).
4. After the batter strikes three balls off the tee, the coach pitches three balls to the batter from a distance of 20 feet.
5. Fielders collect the balls.
6. After several turns, rotate an outfielder to the hitting position.

The fat bat offers a wider surface for striking the ball. Be sure to allow hitters having trouble making contact to hit off the batting tee first before they attempt to hit live pitches. Hitters will probably be successful striking the ball off the batting tee because it is a stationary target. Using whiffle balls allows for lots of repetitions without having to chase the balls long distances.

88. Toss and Hit 

Purpose: To develop eye-hand coordination for striking.

Number of Players: 6
Equipment: 3 baseballs, 3 helmets, 1 bat, 1 game marker
Time: 12 to 15 minutes

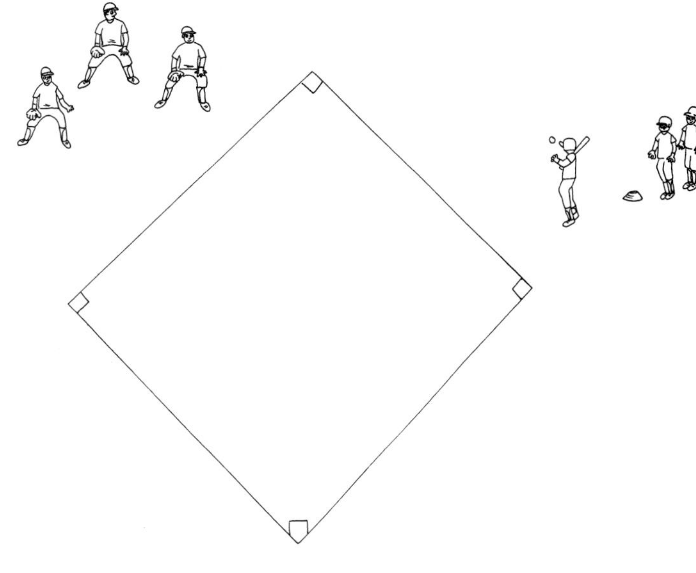

1. Position one batter on the right-field foul line, with two other batters behind a designated safety base (game marker) awaiting their turn.
2. Position three outfielders in left field.
3. The first hitter tosses a ball into the air and strikes it. If the ball is caught in the air, the outfielders receive 5 points.
4. If the ball is caught on the ground, the outfielders receive 1 point.
5. If the outfielders make an error while playing the ball, they lose all of their points.
6. If the hitting team hits the ball over the left-field foul line in the air, they switch roles with the outfielders.
7. The hitters alternate turns.
8. When the outfielders have accumulated 20 points, they switch roles with the hitters.

This is a good outfield hitting drill to use while infielders are practicing special situations in the infield. Emphasize tossing the ball with the left hand (right hand for left-handed hitters), coiling, and uncoiling rhythmically. Beginning players may use fat bats and whiffle balls if contact isn't consistent. Some instances may require a tennis racket and tennis balls. The tennis racket provides a much larger surface for striking the ball. Adjust the outfielders accordingly in these situations.

89. No Stride 

Purpose:
To improve the bat's contact with the ball by reducing the hitter's head movement.
Number of Players:
1
Equipment:
6 safety balls,
1 helmet, 1 bat,
1 batting tee
Time:
3 to 5 minutes

1. Position a batting tee behind the backstop.
2. Draw two lines beside the tee for the batter to position his feet.
3. Instruct the batter to swing without striding, concentrating only on watching the bat striking the ball.
4. Repeat until all balls have been hit.

Batters who have lots of head movement generally make poor contact with the ball. Poor contact with the ball is often caused by overstriding (lunging), which causes the head and hands to drop. As players improve contact without a stride, add the stride but with restrictions.

90. Stride to Line

Purpose:
To develop the batter's concept of transferring weight when hitting.
Number of Players:
1
Equipment:
6 safety balls,
1 helmet,
1 bat,
1 batting tee
Time:
3 to 5 minutes

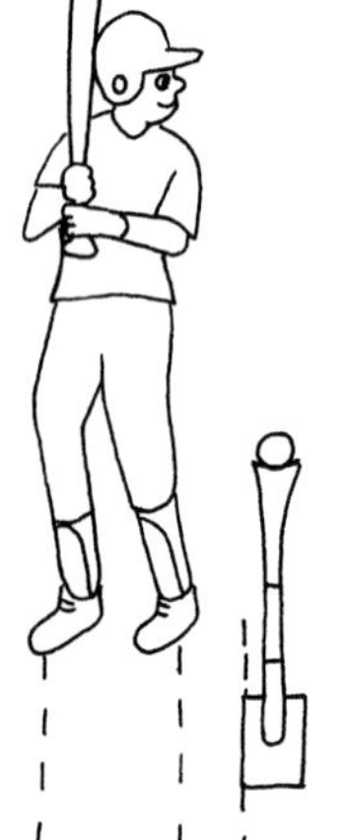

1. Position a batting tee 10 feet behind the backstop.
2. Draw two lines in the dirt to represent the starting position for the hitter (if a grass surface, use chalk or paint) to place her feet. These lines should be about shoulder width apart.
3. Draw a third line 8 inches in front of the line where the front foot would be positioned after striding to hit the ball.
4. Place a ball on the batting tee. Instruct the hitter to push off with her back foot, stepping forward with her front foot and landing on the line when striking the ball.
5. Repeat until all balls have been hit.

The stride is a major component of the hitting technique. Beginning players often have a long stride, which lowers their upper body, including the head. This makes tracking the ball more difficult because of the movement of the eyes, resulting in poor contact. On the other hand, some players strike the ball using all arms and no lower body. This drill helps them transfer weight from their back foot to their front foot, giving them more power. As players develop, encourage pivoting on the back foot, which enables shoulder and hip rotation.

91. Stride to Spot

Purpose: To prevent the batter from bailing out when swinging.

Number of Players: 4
Equipment: 6 safety balls, 1 helmet, 1 bat, 1 batting tee, 3 game spots
Time: 12 to 15 minutes

1. Position a batting tee in the outfield away from the rest of the practice action.
2. Place a game spot on the grass to identify the starting position of the right foot and another for the left foot while engaged in the hitting motion (these spots will be shoulder width apart.)
3. Place a third game spot 8 inches in front of the hitter's front foot (the one that would be closest to the pitcher if it were a game situation).
4. Position a hitter at the batting tee. Have him stand on the right and left game spots.
5. Position three players 100 feet from the batting tee to field balls.
6. The hitter places a ball on the tee and strikes the ball while striding and landing his front foot on the third game spot.
7. The fielders retrieve the ball.
8. Repeat until all balls have been hit.
9. Rotate an outfielder to the hitting position and begin again.

Players bail out when hitting either because they are afraid of the ball or because of poor hitting technique. Placing a game spot that they must land their foot on when hitting will force them to develop proper technique. This drill is similar to the Stride to Line drill (drill 90) except the emphasis is on the direction of the stride and not the length of the stride. After players are comfortable with striding toward the pitcher, repeat the action with the coach pitching.

92. Back Foot Step

Purpose: To eliminate stepping forward with the back foot when swinging.

Number of Players: 1
Equipment: 3 safety balls, 1 helmet, 1 bat, 1 batting tee
Time: 3 to 5 minutes

1. Position the batting tee behind the backstop.
2. Draw a line beside the batting tee to represent where the batter should position his back foot (right foot for right-handed hitters, left foot for left-handed hitters) when hitting.
3. The hitter places a ball on the batting tee and strikes it.
4. A coach checks the position of the back foot and provides any necessary feedback.
5. Repeat until all balls have been hit.

In rare cases, some players step toward the pitcher with the front foot, then step with the back foot, then toward the pitcher with the front foot again before striking the ball (almost like a crow-hop and throw except with a bat). This drill helps reduce this movement. At the end of each swing, have the player check his back foot placement to see if it is still on the line. If several players demonstrate a need for this drill, set it up in the outfield as part of station work.

93. Opposite Side of the Plate

Purpose: To develop the batter's tracking skills.

Number of Players: 5
Equipment: 6 whiffle balls, 2 helmets, 2 whiffle ball bats, 1 game marker
Time: 12 to 15 minutes

1. Position a home plate in the outfield grass.
2. Position a coach 20 feet from home plate. Position three fielders 50 feet from the home plate to collect hit balls.
3. Position one player in a hitting stance on the opposite side of the plate, which would normally be his preferred side. Station another hitter on deck behind a designated safety base (game marker) awaiting his turn.
4. The coach throws a pitch to the hitter, who tries to strike the ball with the bat.
5. If the ball is hit, the appropriate fielder retrieves the ball and returns it to the coach.
6. After six pitches, the hitter assumes a fielding position. The player who was on deck becomes the next hitter. One of the fielders rotates to the on-deck position.
7. Repeat until all players have had a chance to hit.

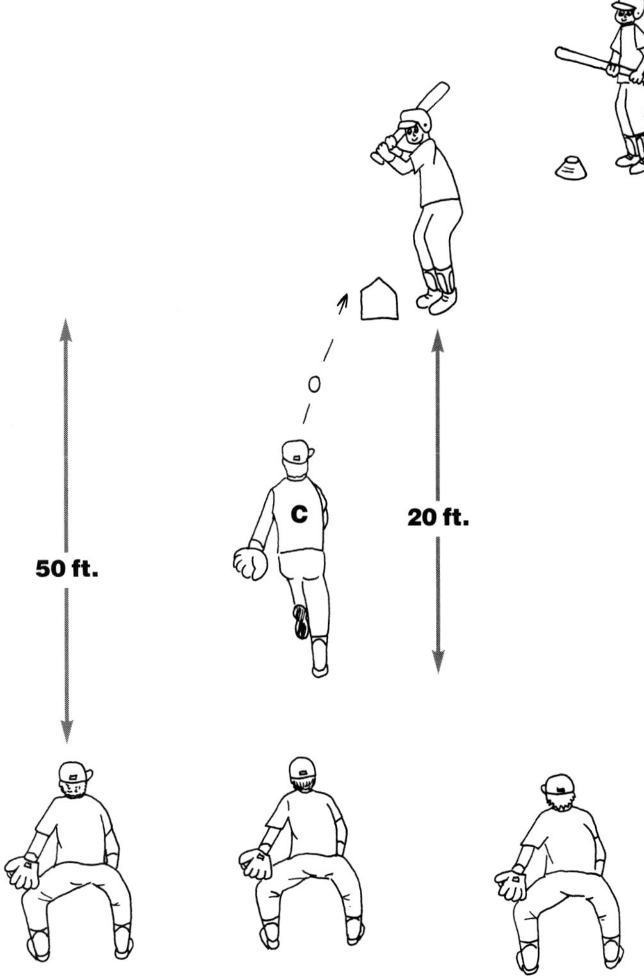

Most players who switch to the opposite side of the plate feel very unnatural trying to hit the ball. This unnatural feeling causes them to concentrate more on watching the ball strike the bat. Using whiffle balls reduces the chance of injury caused by not knowing how to react to a ball thrown at the batter when on the opposite side of the plate.

94. Toss and Swing

Purpose: To develop an efficient swing pattern.

Number of Players: 4
Equipment: 3 baseballs, 4 helmets, 1 bat, 1 game marker, 1 safety net
Time: 12 to 15 minutes

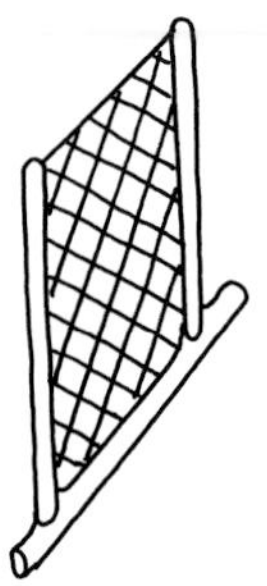

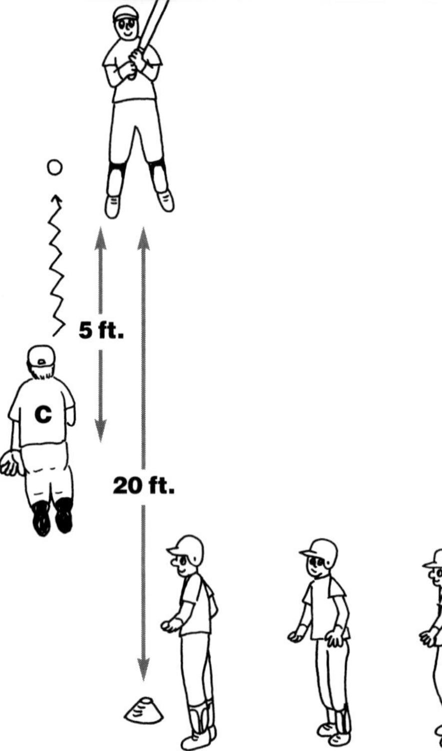

1. Position one player in a hitting position behind and facing the backstop. Place a safety net between the hitter and the backstop.
2. A coach kneels 5 feet from the hitter. Position three players behind a designated safety base (game marker) positioned 20 feet from the hitter.
3. The coach tosses a ball to the hitter.
4. The hitter strikes the ball into the safety net and resets, getting ready for the next toss.
5. After all three balls have been hit, the hitter and two of the three players awaiting their turn behind the coach retrieve the balls while the fourth player quickly positions himself to hit.
6. Repeat, rotating players until all have had a chance to hit.

This drill allows players to participate in a fast-paced activity with lots of repetition. Having players swing at only three pitches then wait for another turn simulates game conditioning, in which they must learn to gather their focus for each at bat. Carefully observe players' positioning and movements to detect flaws and make necessary corrections concerning stride, hip rotation, pivot of the back foot, and so forth. Correct players by breaking the skills down into fundamental parts. Consider giving a visual demonstration followed by verbal clues as players repeat the action.

95. Strike Zone

Purpose: To develop the batter's understanding of the strike zone.

Number of Players: 1
Equipment: 12 baseballs, 1 helmet, 1 bat, 1 safety net
Time: 3 to 5 minutes

1. Position the batter 6 feet away from and facing the backstop. Place a safety net between the hitter and the backstop.
2. A coach kneels 5 feet from the batter.
3. The coach tosses a safety ball from the side. If the ball is in the strike zone, the batter hits it into the safety net.
4. The coach varies the tosses to include balls outside the strike zone, which should not be hit.
5. Repeat using all 12 balls.

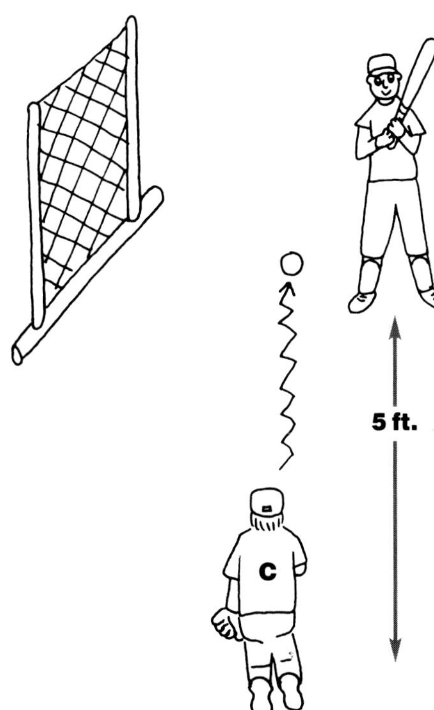

This drill develops discipline and decision making concerning which pitches to hit. It also improves tracking skills, which making good contact with the ball requires. To allow the hitter a chance to be in position to "pull the trigger," drop your throwing hand and then toss the ball.

96. Stop the Hitch

Purpose: To develop a proper swing pattern by the batter.

Number of Players: 4
Equipment: 20 safety balls, 4 helmets, 4 bats, 4 batting tees
Time: 8 to 10 minutes

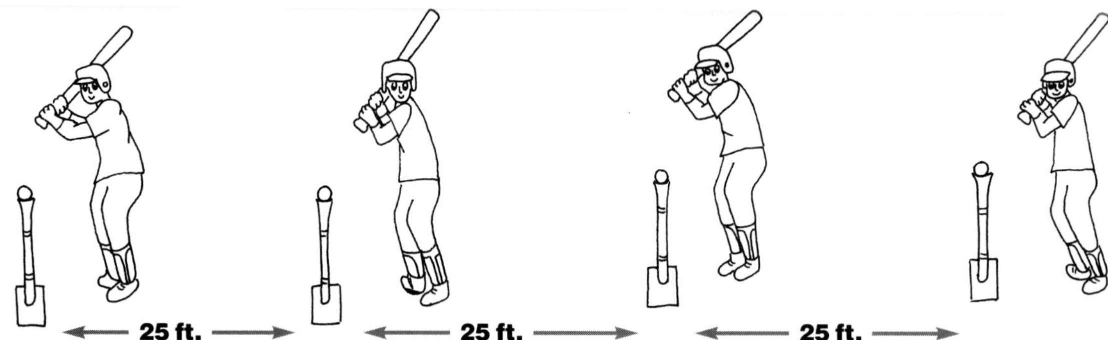

1. Position four batting tees 25 feet apart and a hitter at each batting tee.
2. Hitters place a ball on the tee and assume a hitting stance (feet shoulder width apart, hands back, arms extended).
3. A coach calls out, "Pull."
4. On this command, the hitters pull through with the left arm (right arm for left-handed hitters) as the right arm (left arm for left-handed hitters) follows, allowing the bat to strike the ball.
5. Repeat until all balls have been hit.

This is a perfect opportunity to watch hitters' swing patterns and make corrections. Beginning players very often drop their hands during the swing. Called a hitch, this movement often causes poor contact. Encourage hitters to move from their starting position through the ball without dropping their hands. The bat should be almost parallel with the ground through much of the swing. To help players struggling with this concept, have them start with the bat flat on their shoulder.

97. Pepper

Purpose: To develop the batter's eye-hand coordination for striking.

Number of Players: 5

Equipment: 1 baseball, 1 helmet, 1 bat

Time: 8 to 10 minutes

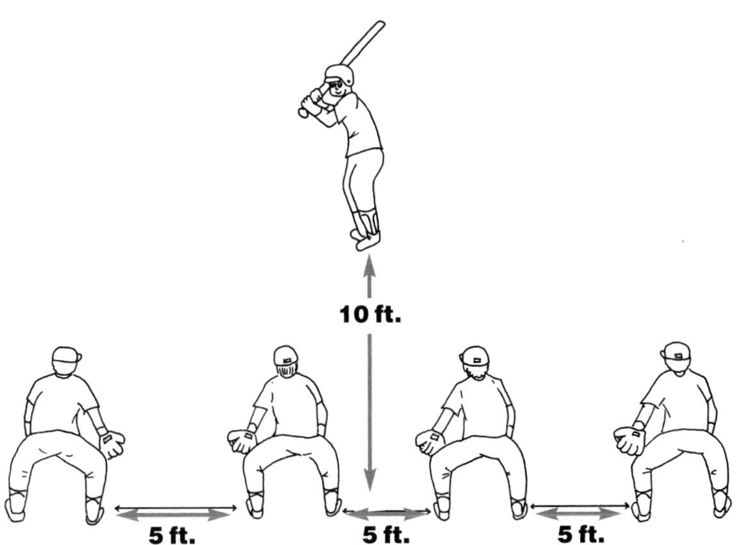

1. Position four players in a line in a "ready" fielding position. Players should be 5 feet apart.
2. Position one player with a bat 10 feet from the players in the line.
3. The first player in line (the player farthest to the batter's left when facing the line) tosses the ball to the batter, who strikes it to the next player in line. Action continues down the line.
4. When the player at the end of the line (to the batter's right) tosses the ball, the batter hits it to the first player in line.
5. If a batter misses a ball or fails to strike it to the proper fielder, the player at the beginning of the line (batter's left) replaces him.
6. The batter who is being replaced takes a place at the end of the line (batter's right).

This fast-moving game of pepper is great for developing tracking skills. Tracking skills relate to the eyes' ability to follow the flight of the ball. In this case, the eyes track the ball until its impact with the bat. Caution batters to take short, nonaggressive swings to reduce injury. Encourage them to "choke up" on the bat to help with bat control and to reduce the speed of the hit ball. Have the players challenge batters by throwing pitches at different levels.

98. Rhythm

Purpose: To develop the batter's technique for putting the body in motion before the pitch.

Number of Players: 5
Equipment: 4 helmets, 4 bats
Time: 5 to 7 minutes

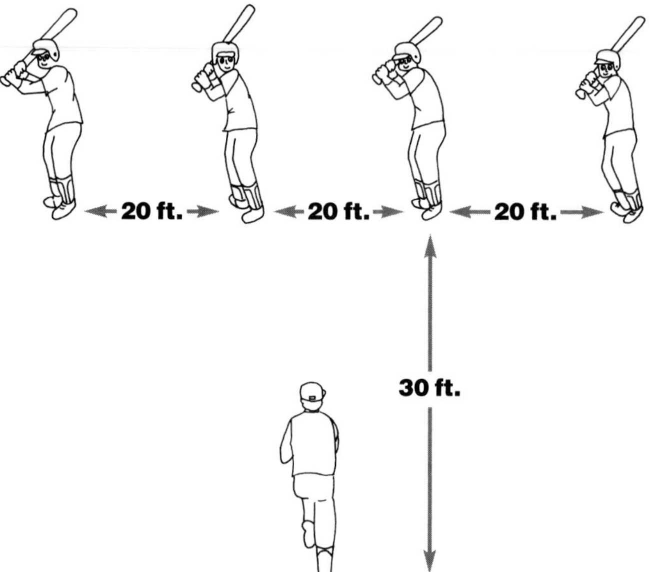

1. Position four batters in a line 20 feet apart from each other.
2. Position another player, acting as pitcher, 30 feet from the batters.
3. As the pitcher winds up to make an imaginary pitch, batters begin to put their bodies in motion for the swing.
4. A coach observes each player, making adjustments as necessary.
5. Repeat.

As the speed of pitches increases at higher levels of play, batters must begin a routine that allows the body to be in motion and the hands to begin the forward movement almost simultaneously with the delivery of the pitch. This routine varies according to player comfort, with some players lifting the front foot, flapping an elbow, or subtly shifting weight from the front to the back foot. Whatever the routine, the bat head should be able to meet the ball without being consistently late. Much like a foul shot in basketball, this routine varies among individuals but should be comfortable and should allow batters to focus on striking the ball. Focus on limited head movement to avoid impairing vision, which could interfere with tracking the ball.

99. Combo Hitting

Purpose: To offer multiple types of hitting practice during the same session.

Number of Players: 16

Equipment: 22 safety balls, 6 whiffle balls, 7 helmets, 3 bats, 1 whiffle ball bat, 1 batting tee, 1 safety net

Time: 60 minutes

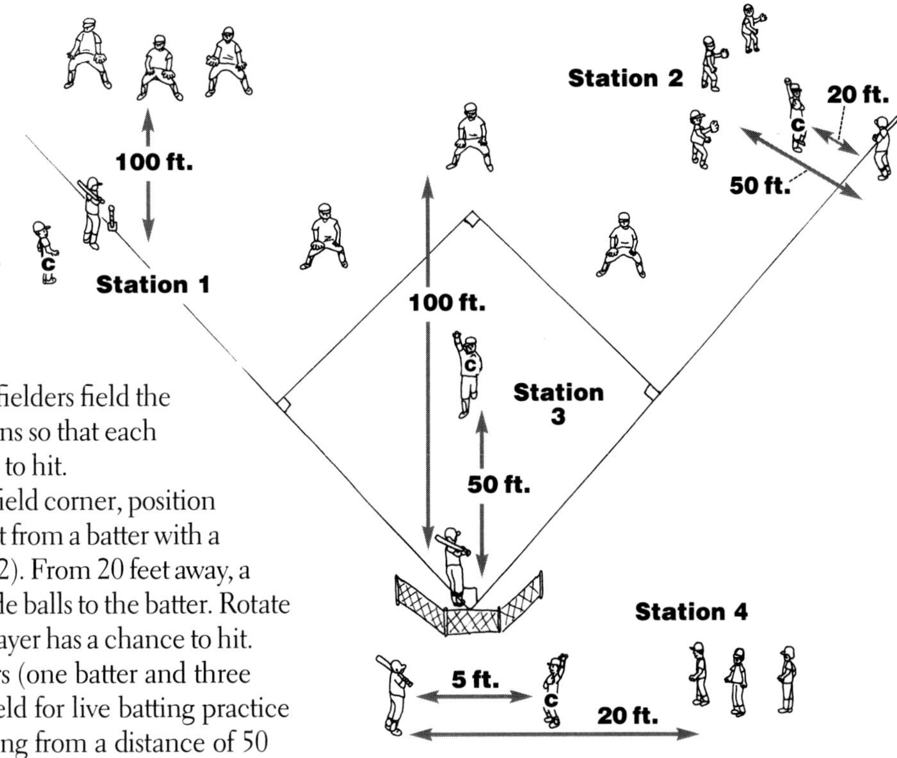

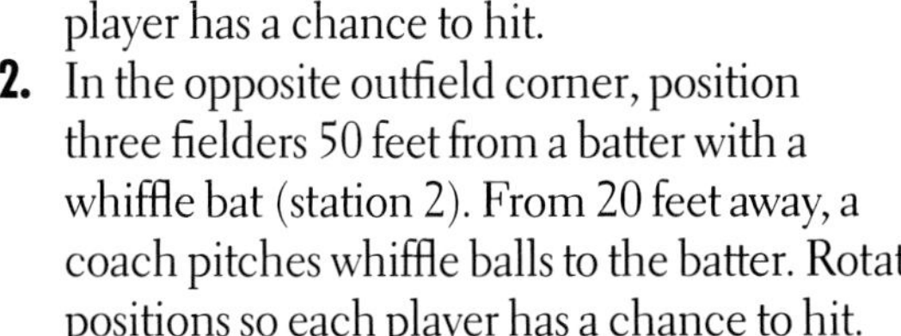

1. Position four players (one batter and three fielders) in the left corner of the outfield with a coach (station 1). Position the fielders 100 feet from the batter. The batter hits six balls off a batting tee and the fielders field the balls. Rotate positions so that each player has a chance to hit.
2. In the opposite outfield corner, position three fielders 50 feet from a batter with a whiffle bat (station 2). From 20 feet away, a coach pitches whiffle balls to the batter. Rotate positions so each player has a chance to hit.
3. Position four players (one batter and three fielders) in the infield for live batting practice with a coach pitching from a distance of 50 feet (station 3). Position the fielders 100 feet from the batter. Allow each player 10 swings and then rotate positions.
4. Position four players behind the backstop with a coach (station 4). One player hits six balls tossed by the coach from a distance of 5 feet into the safety net while the other three players (positioned 20 feet from the batter) await their turn. The next batter steps in as the balls are retrieved. Rotate batters until all have had a chance to hit.
5. After 15 minutes, rotate players to the next station.
6. Repeat until players have rotated through every station.

If possible, recruit parents as assistant coaches to help with multiple stations in batting practice. This allows you, as the head coach, to roam and observe. Confine this drill to younger players because of the limited distance they can strike a ball. If you have access to a batting cage at your field, replace the batting tee with a pitching machine for intermediate players.

CHAPTER 7

Bunting Drills

Bunting is a strategy used to advance runners who are already on base or to allow a hitter to reach base. Players who have mastered the art of bunting can change the outcome of a game. This chapter discusses types of bunts that advance runners, including the sacrifice bunt, the suicide bunt, the safety squeeze, the bunt and run, and the fake bunt and run. The bunting drills are in small- and large-group format, giving players opportunities to develop proper technique concerning footwork, hand and finger placement, angling the bat, and deadening the ball. Bunting for a base hit is distinguished from the other types of bunts. Some of the drills include base runners, while others do not.

All of the drills are designed for intermediate and advanced players. Bunting and bunting strategies shouldn't be presented to beginning players, who are challenged enough by the fundamental skills of throwing, fielding, and hitting. Adding too much structure too soon complicates the game more for them.

Bunting is an important skill for more advanced players to master.

100. Pivoting for a Bunt

Purpose: To teach the proper technique for executing a sacrifice bunt.

Number of Players: 5
Equipment: 4 helmets, 4 bats, 4 game spots
Time: 5 to 7 minutes

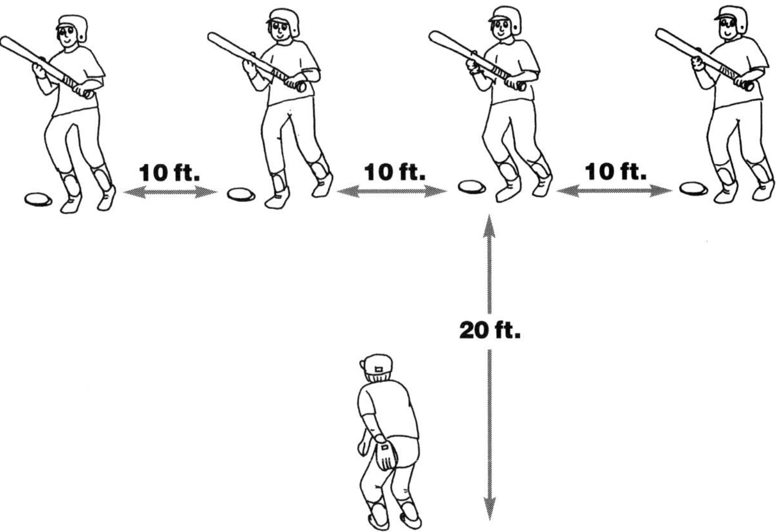

Note key to symbols, page 21

1. Position four game spots (representing home plate) 10 feet apart in a line. Position a batter at each game spot.
2. Position a fifth player 20 feet in front of the line of players to act as pitcher.
3. The pitcher winds up and makes an imaginary throw.
4. As the pitcher moves his arm forward toward what would be release of the ball, the batters "square" to bunt by pivoting, flexing their legs, and moving the bat so that the head of the bat is in front of the game spot representing home plate. The bat head should be slightly elevated.
5. Repeat, with the pitcher alternating between a wind-up and a set position.

Insist that the players pivot, without a lot of foot movement, instead of stepping toward the pitcher with their back foot and swinging their front foot backward in a squared-up position. This action of stepping toward the pitcher makes it too difficult to pivot away from a ball thrown at the hitter. Encourage players to slide their top hand up the bat with all fingers behind the bat. Sliding the hand up the bat allows for more bat control. Placing the fingers behind the bat prevents the ball from striking batters and causing injury.

101. Zone Bunting

Purpose: To develop the batter's concept of where to position a bunted ball.

Number of Players: 4
Equipment: 2 baseballs, 4 helmets, 1 bat, 2 game spots, 1 game marker
Time: 10 to 12 minutes

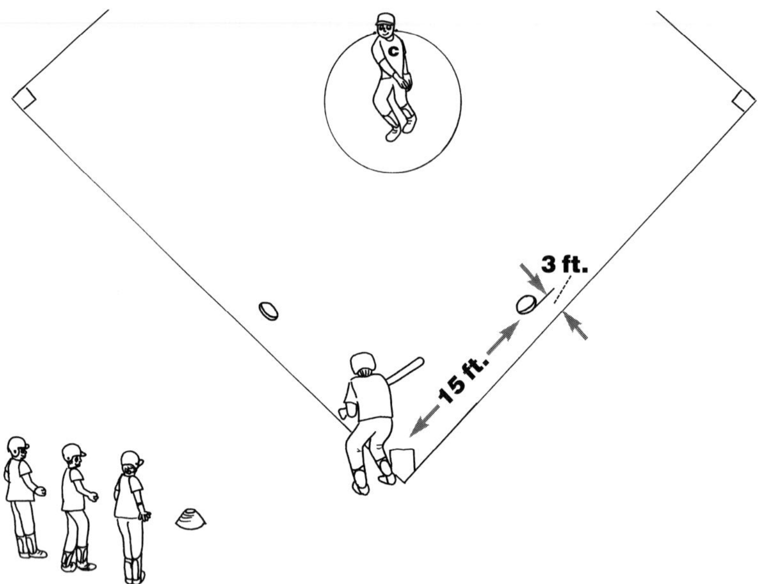

1. Position one batter at home plate. Position the other three players behind a designated safety base (game marker) awaiting their turn.
2. Position two game spots 15 feet from home plate and 3 feet inside the first- and third-base lines.
3. A coach pitches a ball to the batter, who pivots as in a sacrifice bunt and attempts to bunt the ball to either game spot. The batter then runs to first base and returns to take a position behind the safety base.
4. As the second batter moves to the plate, the third player in line retrieves the ball bunted by the first batter.
5. Repeat, rotating players.

Players must learn to recognize where to place a good sacrifice bunt. Visual cues like the game spots help reinforce the concept. Discuss with players ways to deaden the impact of the ball by "giving with the bat" on impact or by contacting the ball with more force by moving the bat head toward the ball on impact.

102. Bunting for a Base Hit

Purpose: To develop the batter's concept of a bunt for a base hit.

Number of Players: 8
Equipment: Catcher's equipment, 1 baseball, 4 helmets, 1 bat, 1 game marker
Time: 12 to 15 minutes

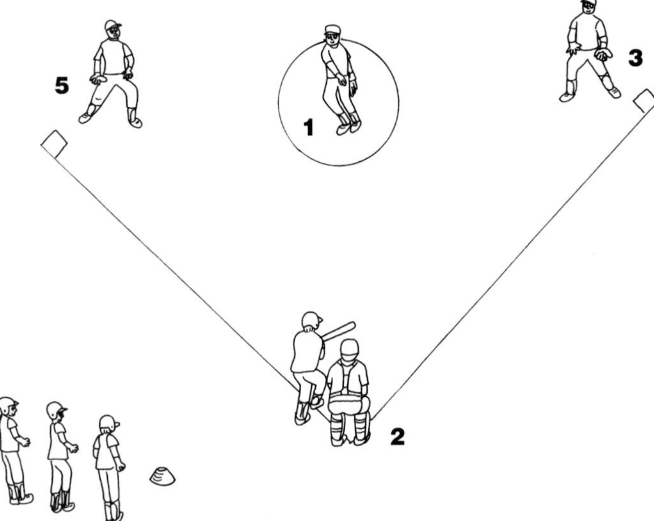

1. Divide players into two teams of four players. Position one team as pitcher, catcher, first-base player, and third-base player.
2. Position one batter at home plate. Station the other batters behind a designated safety base (game marker) awaiting their turn.
3. The pitcher makes a pitch to the batter. As the ball leaves the pitcher's hand, the batter slides his top hand up the bat (fingers behind bat) and in one motion lowers the bat to bunt the ball while beginning to run to first.
4. Fielders play the ball as if in a game situation.
5. Each player on the batting team takes two turns. A team earns 1 point for each successful attempt.
6. The teams switch roles.
7. The winning team is allowed to select the beginning activity for the next day's practice.

The bunt for a base hit strategy is a good offensive weapon for manufacturing runs. The strategy might be influenced by the opponent's position on the field, the opponent's fielding abilities, the pitcher's throwing speed, or the batter's speed, among other factors.

Bunting for a base hit differs from the sacrifice bunt in that the batter does not "square up," thereby showing he is bunting. Bunting for a base hit is more of a surprise strategy. Encourage players not to "show" the bunt by dropping the bat too soon, which alerts fielders that a bunt is on and allows them to move toward the plate sooner. To make this drill gamelike, don't allow the first- and third-base players to play closer than their bases until the ball is pitched.

103. Bunting Game

Purpose: To develop the batter's technique for a sacrifice bunt.

Number of Players: 6
Equipment: 1 baseball, 3 helmets, 1 bat, 9 game markers
Time: 12 to 15 minutes

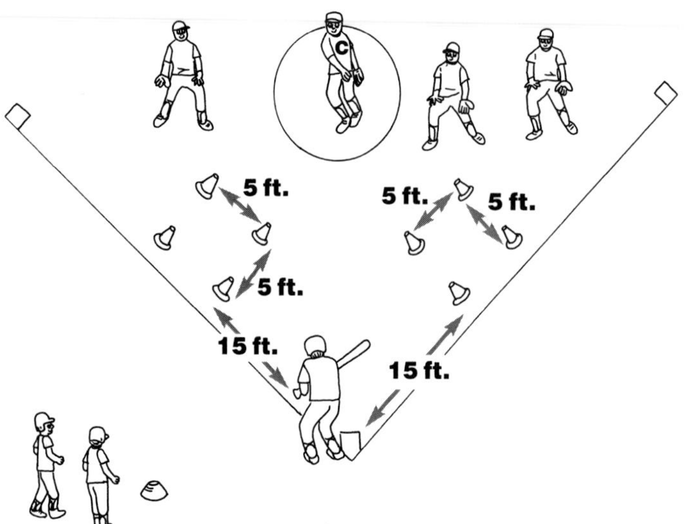

1. Position four game markers to make a 5-foot square 15 feet from home base on the first-base line. Repeat on the third-base line.
2. Divide players into two teams of three players. Position one team in the infield to retrieve balls. Position the other team at home plate, with one player in batting position and the other two behind a designated safety base (game marker) awaiting their turn.
3. A coach pitches to the batter from the regular distance according to league rules.
4. The batter tries to bunt the ball so that it stops rolling in fair territory inside either square.
5. For each ball bunted fair, the bunting team receives 1 point. For each ball bunted in the square, they receive 3 points.
6. The bunting team members rotate after each bunt until each player has had five chances to bunt.
7. Tabulate the bunting team's score.
8. The bunters and fielders change positions. Repeat until every player on the second bunting team has had five chances to bunt.
9. The team with the most points wins.

Many bunting philosophies exist. I like to emphasize pivoting and flexing at the knees with the bat head slightly elevated. Encourage players to "square up" in time to have the head of the bat in front of the plate during the sacrifice bunt. Make sure they learn to bunt only strikes.

104. Safety Squeeze

Purpose: To develop the batter's technique for the safety squeeze bunt.

Number of Players: 9
Equipment: Catcher's equipment, 3 baseballs, 5 helmets, 1 bat
Time: 18 to 20 minutes

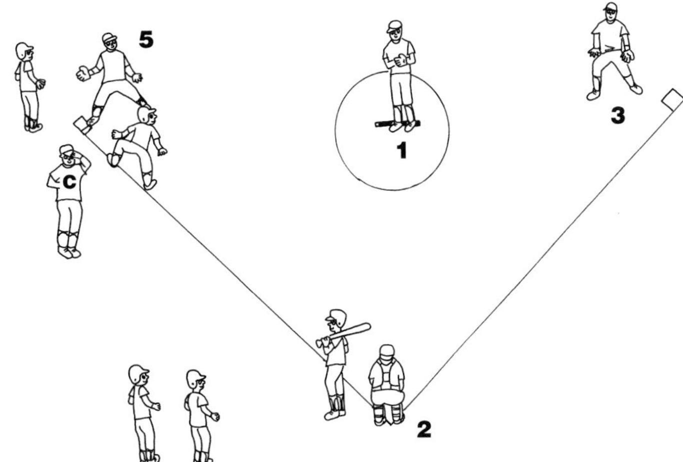

1. Position one batter at home plate with a catcher. Station a second batter on deck awaiting his turn and a third batter to collect foul balls.
2. Position a runner on third base and another runner outside of third base awaiting his turn. Station a coach in the third-base coach's box.
3. Position a pitcher, catcher, first-base player, and third-base player as infielders.
4. The batter steps out of the batter's box to receive the safety squeeze signal from a coach standing in the third-base coach's box. The batter and base runner acknowledge the signal.
5. The pitcher makes a pitch to the batter, who squares as the ball is released and bunts it.
6. The base runner at third base takes his lead but doesn't begin to run home until the ball is bunted toward the ground.
7. The fielders try to make a play at home or, if home isn't possible, at first base.
8. After the play ends, the batter rotates to the third-base side to become a runner.
9. The second batter becomes the hitter.
10. The third batter, who was collecting foul balls, becomes the new second batter. The base runner from third base becomes the new third batter.
11. Repeat, rotating positions until all players have had a chance to bunt.

Encourage batters to bunt only strikes to help avoid popping the ball up. The batter doesn't protect the runner by "bunting all pitches" in this situation because the runner isn't in jeopardy of being thrown out at the plate (he waits to break home until he sees the ball bunted toward the ground).

105. Suicide Bunt 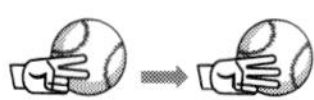

Purpose: To develop the batter's suicide bunt technique.

Number of Players: 8
Equipment: Catcher's equipment, 3 baseballs, 6 helmets, 1 bat
Time: 12 to 15 minutes

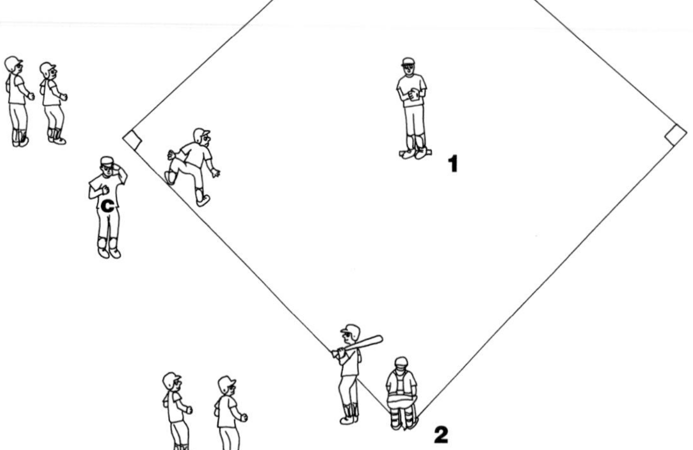

1. Position one batter at home plate with a catcher. Position another on deck awaiting his turn and a third batter to collect foul balls.
2. Position a base runner on third base and a pitcher. Position two other base runners outside the third-base line ready to take a turn running to home. Station a coach in the third-base coach's box.
3. The batter steps out of the batting box to receive a signal from the third-base coach. The batter and base runner acknowledge the signal.
4. The batter squares as the ball is released, bunts the ball toward first base, and then runs to first.
5. The base runner takes her lead and then begins to run home as soon as the pitcher's arm begins moving forward to release the ball.
6. The next hitter hustles to the batter's box and repeats the action.
7. After all hitters have had three chances to bunt, rotate the hitters with the base runners.

The suicide bunt is basically a sacrifice bunt in which the batter waits to square his bat at about the same time the ball is released instead of "showing" the bunt early as in the basic sacrifice bunt. Showing the bunt early could lead to a pitchout or even to throwing at the batter. The batter and the base runner can acknowledge that they have received the signal by something as simple as putting their hands on their hips or rubbing their hands together. Bunting the ball toward first base makes it more difficult for the pitcher, especially a right-hander, to make a play at the plate. Encourage batters to bunt all pitchers regardless of their location.

106. Bunt and Run 

Purpose: To develop the batter's bunt-and-run technique.

Number of Players: 8

Equipment: Catcher's equipment, 3 baseballs, 4 helmets, 1 bat

Time: 12 to 15 minutes

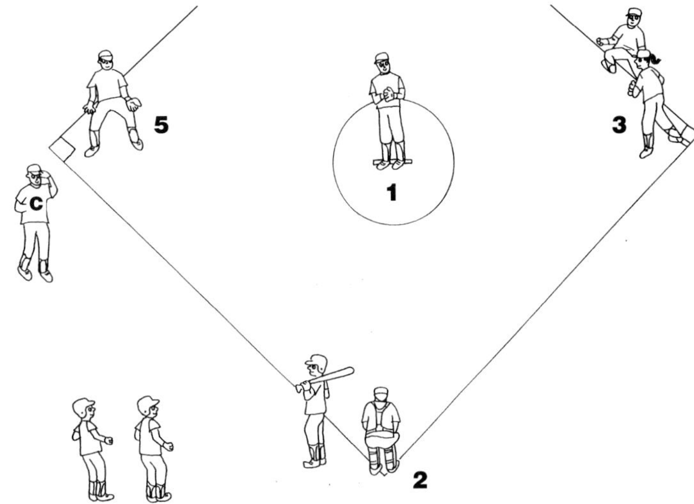

1. Position a base runner at first base and a batter at home plate. Position two other batters in the on-deck circle awaiting their turn.
2. Position a first-base player, third-base player, pitcher, and catcher at their defensive positions. Station a coach in the third-base coach's box.
3. The batter at home plate steps out of the batter's box and looks for the third-base coach to give the bunt signal.
4. The base runner at first takes his lead.
5. After the pitcher assumes the set position, just prior to delivery to the plate, the batter squares to bunt.
6. The base runner increases his lead slightly as the ball is delivered to the plate.
7. If the ball is bunted on the ground, the base runner sprints toward second base, then jogs around third and becomes a bunter. The bunter sprints to first and then becomes the new base runner.
8. Fielders try to throw the batter out at first base.
9. Repeat with a new batter.
10. Switch batters and fielders after each batter bunts three times.

Insist that batters step out of the box and look for the signal on each pitch. Base runners should be looking for the coach's signal while on the base. Encourage base runners to take a two-stride lead as the pitcher assumes the set position. Be sure to emphasize to base runners that they don't move to second base until they see the ball being bunted on the ground. This helps avoid either getting doubled off base if the ball is popped up or being pulled off base if the ball is missed.

107. Fake Bunt and Run

Purpose: To develop the batter's technique for the fake bunt and run.

Number of Players: 11
Equipment: Catcher's equipment, 1 baseball, 5 helmets, 1 bat
Time: 18 to 20 minutes

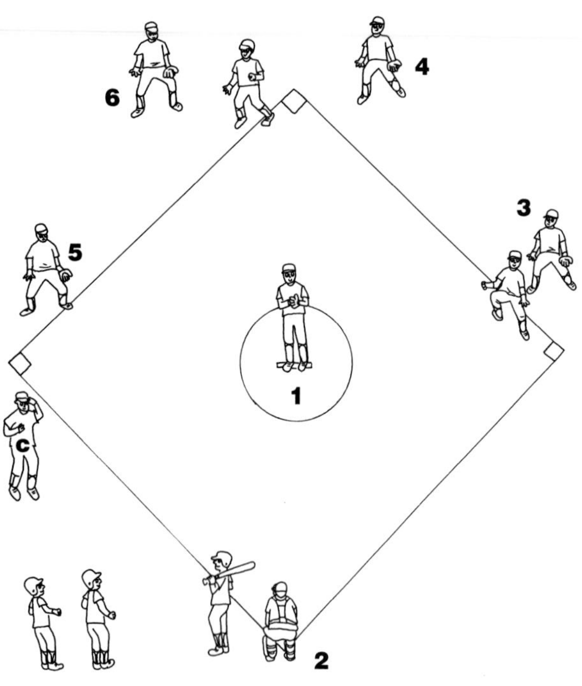

1. Position base runners at first and second base and a batter at home plate. Position two other batters in the on-deck circle awaiting their turn.
2. Position defensive players so that all infield positions, including pitcher and catcher, are occupied. Station a coach in the third-base coach's box.
3. The batter steps out of the box and looks for the third-base coach's signal.
4. Base runners take their leads.
5. As soon as the pitcher begins his motion to the plate from the set position, the base runners sprint to the next base.
6. The batter squares as the pitcher begins the motion to the plate. The batter should have his bat out in front of the plate, parallel to the ground.
7. As the ball is delivered, the batter moves the head of the bat backward toward the catcher on the same level the ball is traveling, being careful not to make contact with the ball.
8. The catcher attempts to throw one of the runners out.
9. The runner who was moving to third moves to the on-deck circle to become a batter.
10. The player who batted moves to first base to become a runner.
11. A new batter steps in and the action is repeated.

The fake bunt and run is used to create movement by infielders and to distort the catcher's vision. The combination of player movement and distorted vision is intended to lead to a defensive breakdown, enabling runners to advance to the next base. This play works best with runners at first and second base with fewer than 2 outs.

CHAPTER 8

Baserunning Drills

Baserunning is an important element of baseball. Teams that limit the amount of baserunning errors they commit give themselves opportunities to score more runs and have big innings.

The baserunning drills in this chapter help develop baserunning technique for hitters, base runners advancing on a hit ball or a bunted ball, base runners tagging on a fly ball, and base runners who are stealing. The chapter also includes drills for specialty situations, including running through first base without leaping, watching the coach when a batted ball isn't in sight of the runner, taking leads using the slide step, and getting a good start when stealing using the crossover step.

The drills are designed primarily for intermediate and advanced players. The first drill, however, does develop beginning players' technique for running to first after a batted ball. Because beginning players don't need a lot of structure in their game, they shouldn't have bunting and stealing techniques presented to them. All of their efforts should be concentrated on developing fundamental skills without being burdened with complicated rules of the game.

The drills involving stealing should be used with advanced players only. Stealing bases is inappropriate for players under age 11, who generally do not have the arm strength to throw runners out. Often, in leagues that allow stealing below age 11, coaches instruct their catchers to hold the ball rather than taking a chance of throwing the ball away when trying to throw a runner out at second base. This creates a system of built-in failure for these players, as well as destroys opportunities for fielders to make plays at bases other than first base, because typically a batter will walk, steal second, steal third, and many times, steal home. Instead, institute a no-walk (if a player gets 4 balls, he must hit off a batting tee), no-steal modification to best meet the needs of the players. This benefits fielders by giving them more opportunities to field batted balls (e.g., to get a force-out at second base), benefits catchers by reducing feelings of inadequacy from not being able to throw a ball accurately all the way to second base, and allows base runners to make decisions concerning baserunning with batted balls. There will be plenty of opportunities to teach stealing skills after age 10.

When using the baserunning drills in this chapter, create a safe environment by having all base runners wear protective helmets.

108. Running to First

Purpose: To develop the base runner's technique for running to first base.

Number of Players: 9
Equipment: 1 baseball, 3 helmets, 1 fungo bat
Time: 8 to 10 minutes

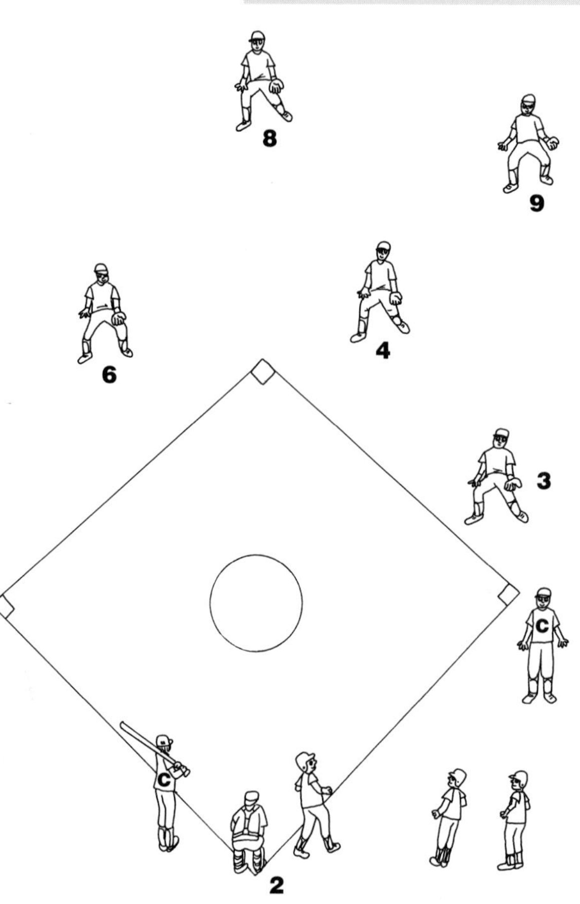

1. Position a first-base player, second-base player, shortstop, center fielder, and right fielder in their fielding positions.
2. Position three base runners at home plate with a catcher and a coach to hit fungoes.
3. Position another coach in the first-base coach's box.
4. The coach at home plate hits the ball. If it is hit on the ground to an infielder, the first-base coach gives a verbal cue to the runner to run as hard as she can through first base.
5. If the ball is hit through the infield, the first-base coach instructs the base runner to "take a turn" then either "go" or "come back."
6. After the play, the runner moves to the end of the line of base runners at home plate.
7. After each base runner has taken a second turn, she exchanges places with one of the fielders.

Encourage runners to run through the base and not leap to get there on a ball hit to the infielders. Balls that are hit to the outfield should be considered a chance for a double. Insist that base runners run hard as soon as the ball is hit and take the turn at first base aggressively, listening for the coach. If the ball is hit to right field or right center, base runners should be able to look and find the ball. This helps their decision making.

109. Go/Back Base Running

Purpose: To develop the base runner's technique for taking a lead and breaking for second or returning to first.

Number of Players: 6
Equipment: 1 baseball, 1 helmet
Time: 10 to 12 minutes

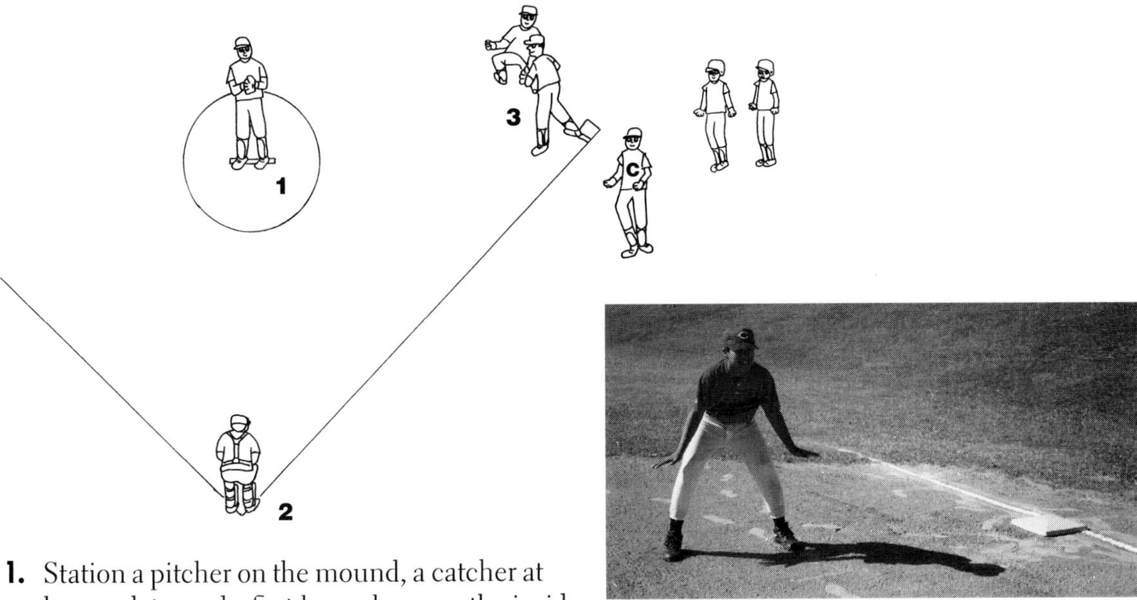

Taking a lead.

1. Station a pitcher on the mound, a catcher at home plate, and a first-base player on the inside of first base where he would position himself to hold a runner on base.
2. Position a base runner on first base, two extra base runners in foul territory, and a coach in the first-base coach's box.
3. As the pitcher comes to the set position, the base runner takes a two-stride lead.
4. If the pitcher throws to first base, the coach yells, "Back!"
5. If the pitcher throws to the catcher, the base runner takes a crossover step and runs hard to second base.
6. Repeat with the other base runners.

Instruct base runners that when taking their two-stride lead, they should use sliding steps without crossing their feet. Crossing their feet will complicate any potential return to first base. When breaking for second base, base runners should use a crossover step, bringing the left foot past the right foot while simultaneously pivoting on the right foot. When returning to first base, runners should dive and extend a hand to the outfield side of first base. When doing so, they should turn their head to face the outfield. This helps prevent being struck in the face with an errant throw.

110. Crossover Tag

Purpose: To develop the base runner's crossover step technique.

Number of Players: 3
Equipment: 3 helmets, 2 game markers
Time: 5 to 7 minutes

1. Position base runners at the beginning of a 90-foot straight line formed by game markers. The base runners should be spaced 5 feet apart.
2. On a coach's first signal, base runners assume a ready position by flexing their hips and knees and extending their arms and hands to the side.
3. On the coach's second signal, the runners execute a crossover step and run as fast as they can, trying to tap the runner in front of them.
4. Change positions of the runners so that the runner who was at the end of the line of players is now at the beginning of the line.
5. Repeat.

Developing an effective crossover step saves base runners precious time when attempting to steal. Encourage them to cross the left foot over the right while simultaneously pivoting on the right foot.

Note key to symbols, page 21

111. Stealing First and Third

Purpose: To develop the base runner's technique for stealing first and third base.

Number of Players: 10
Equipment: Catcher's equipment, 1 baseball, 4 helmets
Time: 12 to 15 minutes

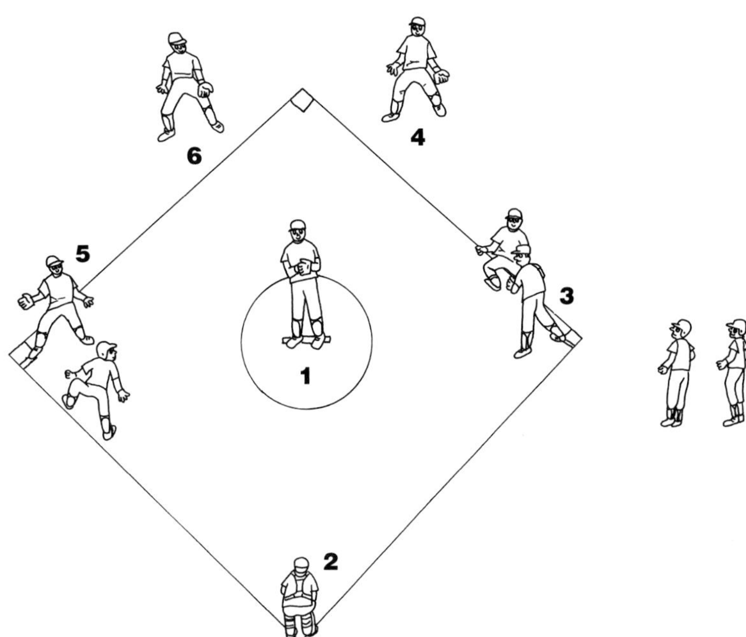

1. Position a player in every infield position, including pitcher and catcher.
2. Position base runners on first and third base. Position two extra base runners by the first-base coach's box awaiting their turn.
3. The pitcher raises his arms to go in the set position. At the same time, the runner on first takes his lead.
4. As the pitcher throws to the catcher, the runner on first breaks for second.
5. The catcher throws to second base.
6. As the ball goes past the pitcher, the runner on third breaks for home.
7. Repeat, with the next base runner in line taking a turn.

Many defensive plays can be used to combat the first- and third-base steal. Sometimes the catcher fakes a throw to second and throws instead to third, throws hard back to the pitcher, or throws directly to a middle infielder who has charged toward home when the runner at first broke for second. It is the responsibility of the runner at third base to make sure the ball passes the pitcher before the runner breaks for home plate. The runner at third must have a good lead but not so much as to be picked off by the catcher.

112. First- to Third-Base Running 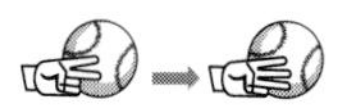

Purpose: To develop the base runner's technique for moving from first to third base on a ball hit to the outfield.

Number of Players: 10
Equipment: 1 baseball, 4 helmets, 1 fungo bat
Time: 12 to 15 minutes

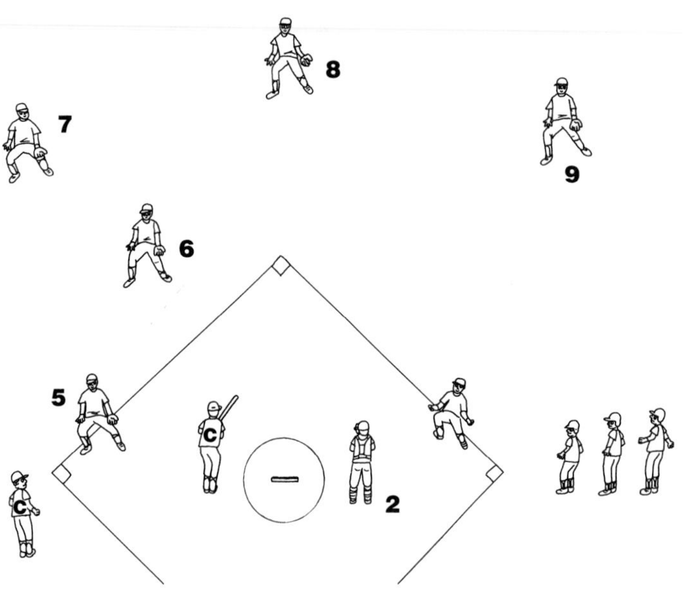

1. Position a runner on first base and three other runners by the first-base coach's box awaiting their turn.
2. Position fielders at shortstop, third base, and all outfield positions.
3. Station a coach on the pitcher's mound to hit fungoes. Station another coach in the third-base coach's box.
4. The base runner at first assumes a two-stride lead.
5. As the coach on the pitcher's mound hits the ball to the outfield, the base runner runs hard to second base.
6. About halfway to second base, the base runner looks at the third-base coach, who either gives her a hand signal to stop at second base or waves her on to third. The base runner follows the coach's signal.
7. The base runner moves to the end of the line of runners.
8. Repeat with the next runner.

Base runners who have the ball hit in front of them have more information about their next decision. If the ball is hit behind them—to right or right center—they need the third-base coach's help to make the best decision. This often occurs in hit-and-run situations in which a right-hander hits behind (to the right side of) base runners. The key is to run hard and look. As runners approach third base, the coach gives a hand signal either to stand up or to get down and slide. Usually, the coach kneels when giving the signal to slide.

113. Runner on Second 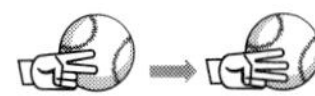

Purpose: To develop the base runner's technique with a runner on second and fewer than 2 outs.

Number of Players: 5
Equipment: 1 baseball, 1 helmet, 1 fungo bat
Time: 8 to 10 minutes

1. Position a base runner at second base. Station a second base runner on the outfield side of second base awaiting his turn.
2. Position a shortstop and second-base player in fielding position. Position a catcher to catch balls for a coach, who will be hitting fungoes.
3. The runner at second base takes a lead.
4. The coach hits a ground ball to the shortstop or second-base player.
5. If the ball is hit to the shortstop, the runner goes back to second base. If the ball is hit to the second-base player, the runner goes to third base.
6. Repeat with the other base runner.
7. After five repetitions, a base runner switches positions with an infielder.

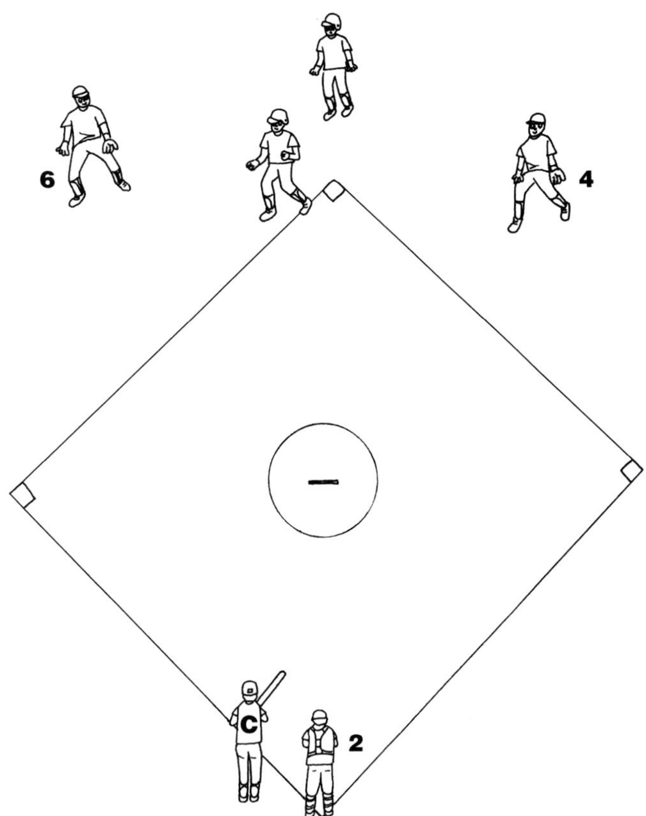

This is a situational drill in which a runner is on second base with fewer than 2 outs. Making good decisions in a situation like this helps prevent giving up an out and getting a runner out of scoring position.

114. Third-Base Tagging

Purpose: To develop the base runner's technique for tagging at third base on a fly ball to the outfield.

Number of Players: 8
Equipment: 1 baseball, 3 helmets, 1 fungo bat
Time: 10 to 12 minutes

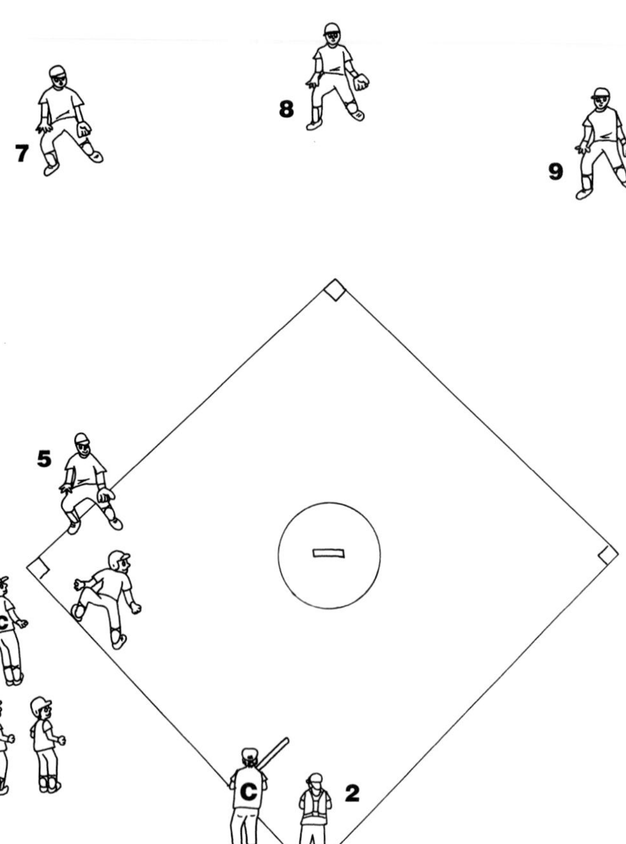

1. Position players in all outfield positions and at third base and catcher.
2. Position a coach at home plate to hit fungoes and another coach in the third-base coach's box.
3. Position a runner on third base. Station two more base runners outside the third-base coach's box awaiting their turn.
4. The runner at third base takes his lead.
5. The coach at home plate hits a fly ball to one of the outfielders.
6. As soon as the ball is hit, the runner at third returns to the base.
7. When the ball is caught, the third-base coach tells the runner to "go" or "stay."
8. Rotate in a new base runner and repeat.

Vary the depth of the fly balls to create a range of possibilities for the base runners. Encourage base runners to return to third base on any ball hit to the outfield, look toward home and not at the ball, and wait to hear the coach's command.

115. Running with the Bases Loaded

Purpose: To develop the base runner's technique for a base hit with bases loaded.

Number of Players: 14
Equipment: 1 baseball, 5 helmets, 1 fungo bat
Time: 18 to 20 minutes

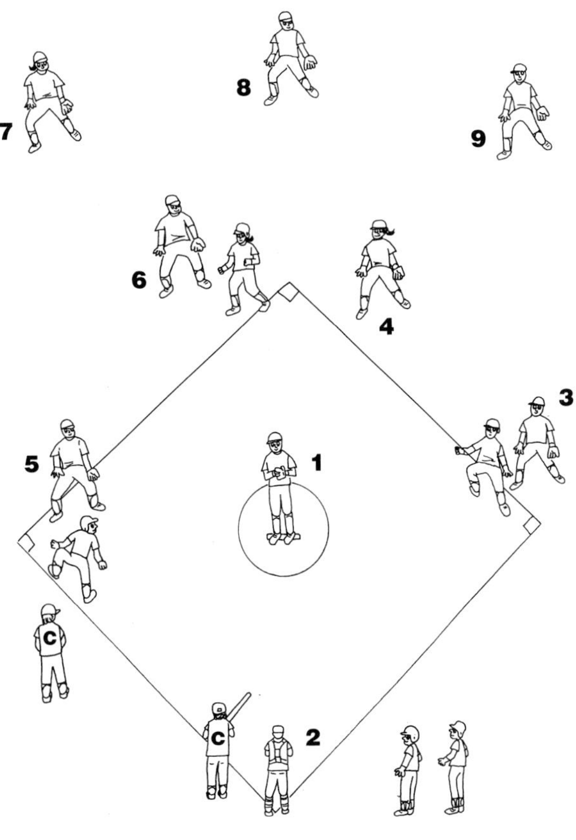

1. Position players at all fielding positions. Station a coach at home plate to hit and another coach in the third-base coach's box.
2. Position runners at first, second, and third base. Station two extra base runners next to home plate awaiting their turn.
3. The runners on base take their leads.
4. The coach hits the ball in the air to the outfield.
5. As soon as the ball is hit, the runner at third goes back to third, and the runner at second either goes halfway or, if the ball is deep enough, tags from second. The runner on first goes halfway to second.
6. Use the extra runners to load the bases again. This time, the coach hits the ball to the outfield on the ground.
7. The runner from third scores.The runner from second looks to the third-base coach, who has moved partway down the third-base line, for a hand signal whether to stop at third or continue home.
8. The runner on first watches the runner ahead of him and any signal from the third-base coach, who is working his way back to third base.
9. Load the bases and repeat.

Vary hitting fly balls and ground balls so that runners understand their responsibilities for each. Runners going halfway on fly balls must understand that if the ball is hit shallow, they can't go quite as far off base or they might get picked off. Insist that runners have their heads up and be looking at the third-base coach.

CHAPTER 9

Lead-Up Games

The lead-up games presented in this chapter are modified versions of the traditional baseball game that are intended for beginning and intermediate players. All of the games involve the development of hitting and fielding techniques. In some of the games, baserunning requirements and the methods used for earning outs vary from the traditional game.

These modifications allow players more opportunities to be involved in the action because teams consist of five or fewer players. Having a small-sided format means that fewer people share more responsibility and thus have more opportunities for hitting, fielding, and making decisions.

These games have been developed specifically for beginning and intermediate players by modifying the distance to bases; the size, weight, and consistency of the ball; the size and weight of the bat; and the number of times a player bats per inning. Safety precautions include the use of a batting tee, a safety base, and a safety ball. Players are allowed to strike a ball off a batting tee. This allows players to develop a swing pattern using a stationary object, which helps build confidence without the fear of being struck by a pitched ball.

Using modified games means that more games can be played simultaneously. If enough backstops aren't available to accommodate every group of players, institute safety precautions so that players won't be struck with thrown bats.

In each of the games, players on the hitting teams are required to stand behind a safety base placed 30 feet behind the batting team. Make a rule that no one is allowed to touch the bat until everyone on the team is behind the safety base. Then the first person can move to the batting tee to take a turn. I use this method when working with beginning players. Often, I have one game being played in the infield and two other games being played in the outfield (one in right field and one in left field).

The type of ball used for these games varies according to the skill level of the players. I have used sponge, gator-skinned, whiffle, and canvas-covered modified baseballs. Generally, the younger the players, the bigger and lighter the ball and bat should be.

Lead-Up Game 1 

Purpose: To develop hitting and fielding skills in a small-sided format.

Number of Players: 6

Equipment: 1 safety ball, 3 helmets, 1 bat, 1 batting tee, 2 game markers

Time: 18 to 20 minutes

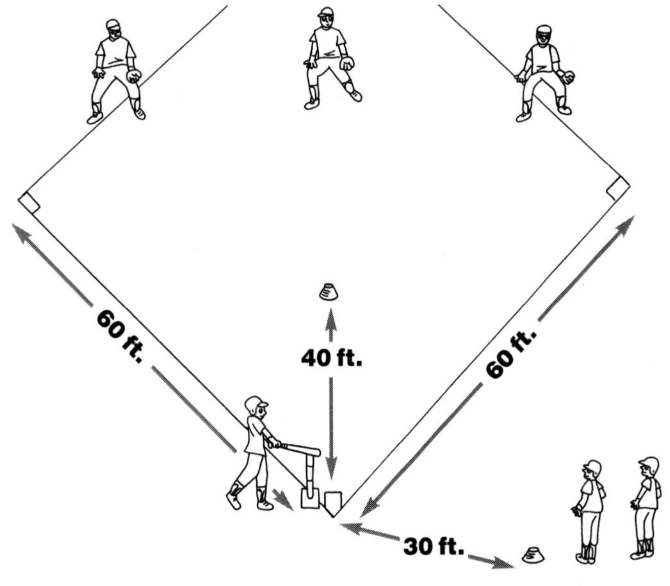

1. Position side bases so that they are 60 feet from home plate on what would normally be the first- and third-base sides of the field.
2. Position a game marker 40 feet from home base in a line toward what would normally be second base.
3. Divide players into two teams. One team will hit while the other team fields.
4. Line up the hitting team behind a designated safety base (game marker) positioned 30 feet behind the batting tee. Space the fielding team in the field.
5. The first hitter strikes the ball off the batting tee, runs around the game marker, and returns to home base.
6. The fielders retrieve the ball and try to touch one of the side bases before the hitter can touch home base. They aren't allowed to touch the game marker.
7. If the hitter returns home safely, the hitter's team scores 1 run. If the fielder successfully touches one of the side bases first, the hitter is out.
8. After each player on the hitting team has taken two turns, the teams switch roles.

Note key to symbols, page 21

This will be the first experience for many players of hitting the ball and then running to a base or fielding the ball and returning it to a base. Thus the game is designed to be as uncomplicated as possible for both hitters and fielders. Allow players to concentrate on hitting and fielding techniques without being burdened with specific fielding positions and the complicated rules of baseball. It's enough to expect the players to understand that when they hit the ball they run to a base (the game marker, in this case) and that when they field a ball they try to return it to a base the fastest way possible.

Lead-Up Game 2

Purpose: To develop hitting and fielding skills in a small-sided format.

Number of Players: 6
Equipment: 1 safety ball, 3 helmets, 1 bat, 1 batting tee, 4 game markers
Time: 18 to 20 minutes

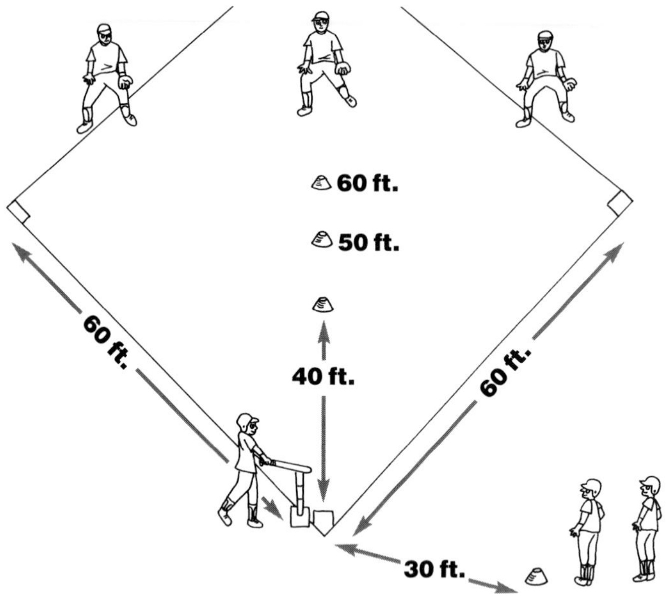

1. Position side bases 60 feet from home base on what would normally be the first- and third-base sides of the field.
2. Position three game markers, one 40, one 50, and one 60 feet from home base on a line toward what would normally be second base. Place a designated safety base (game marker) 30 feet behind home plate. The batting team will stand behind this safety base.
3. Divide players into two teams. One team will hit while the other team fields.
4. Line up the hitting team behind the safety base. Space the fielding team in the field.
5. The first hitter strikes the ball off the batting tee and decides which of the game markers to run around before returning to home base. If the hitter runs around the first marker and returns home safely, he scores 1 run; the second marker, 2 runs; and the third marker, 5 runs.
6. The fielders retrieve the ball and try to touch one of the side bases before the batter can touch home base. If they are successful, the batter is out.
7. After each player on the batting team takes two turns, the teams switch roles.

Players will be tempted to earn 5 runs for their team by running around the last game marker each time they hit the ball. Encourage them, instead, to decide which base to run around according to how far they hit the ball. This should lead to better baserunning decisions during regular games.

Lead-Up Game 3

Purpose: To develop hitting and fielding skills in a small-sided format.

Number of Players: 8
Equipment: 1 safety ball, 4 helmets, 1 bat, 1 batting tee, 1 game marker
Time: 18 to 20 minutes

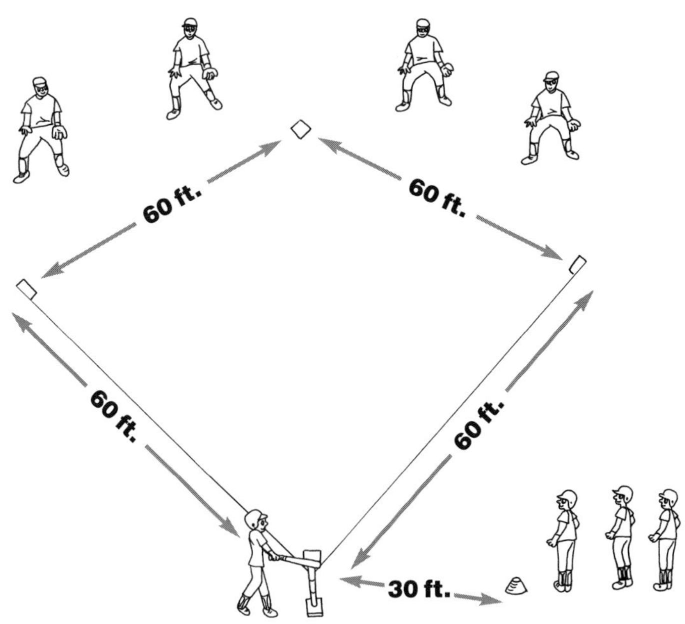

1. Position home plate and bases to make a diamond shape. Bases should be 60 feet apart.
2. Position a designated safety base (game marker) 30 feet behind the batting tee. The batting tee should be situated about 3 feet behind home plate.
3. Divide the players into two teams of four players.
4. Position the batting team behind the safety base. Place the fielding team in the field.
5. Play the game using regular baseball rules.
6. Each team is allowed to score 8 runs each at bat or commit 3 outs. When either occurs, the teams switch batting and fielding roles and begin again.

This small-sided version of the real game of baseball allows players more hitting and fielding opportunities because each team has only four players. Using a batting tee helps develop hitting technique without fear of being struck by the ball. As players progress, increase the level of difficulty by giving them a choice of hitting off the tee or having a coach pitch to them. When appropriate, replace the coach with a player acting as pitcher.

Lead-Up Game 4 

Purpose: To develop hitting and fielding skills in a small-sided format.

Number of Players: 10
Equipment: 1 safety ball, 5 helmets, 1 bat, 1 batting tee, 1 game marker
Time: 18 to 20 minutes

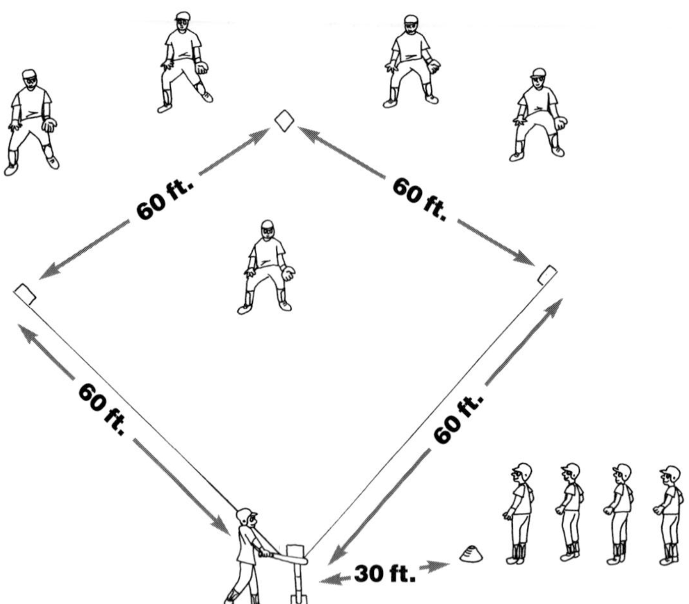

1. Position home plate and bases to make a diamond shape. Bases should be 60 feet apart.
2. Position a designated safety base (game marker) 30 feet behind the batting tee. The batting tee should be situated about 3 feet behind home plate.
3. Divide the players into two teams of five players.
4. Position the batting team behind the safety base. Place the fielding team in the field.
5. Play the game using regular baseball rules with these exceptions:
   - there are no force-outs
   - more than one base runner can be on base at any time
   - base runners may run from third base to home and continue to first base
6. Switch teams after 10 runs have been scored or 3 outs have been made.

This is a fast-paced game with lots of opportunities for developing hitting and fielding techniques. Players also have numerous decision-making opportunities concerning baserunning. In a regular game of baseball, baserunning decisions are based primarily on the location of the ball, the position of teammates on bases, and the quality of the opponents. In this game, the location of the ball and the quality of the opponent are used to make decisions concerning baserunning.

Lead-Up Game 5

Purpose: To develop hitting and fielding skills in a small-sided format.

Number of Players: 7
Equipment: 1 safety ball, 3 helmets, 1 bat, 1 batting tee, 1 game marker
Time: 18 to 20 minutes

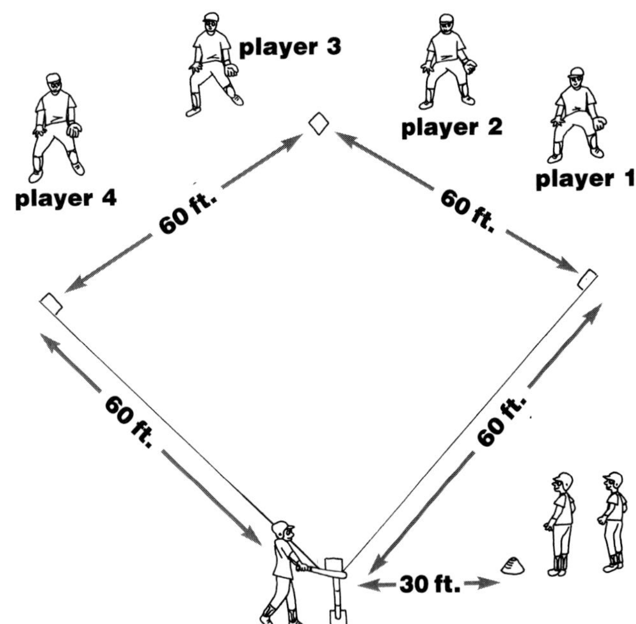

1. Position home plate and bases to make a diamond shape. Bases should be 60 feet apart.
2. Position a designated safety base (game marker) 30 feet behind the batting tee. The batting tee should be situated about 3 feet behind home plate.
3. Divide players into two teams: one team of four fielders and one team of three hitters.
4. Position the batting team behind the safety base. Place the fielding team in the field.
5. Number the fielders 1 through 4.
6. Play the game using regular baseball rules with these exceptions:
    - if a base runner is declared out, he takes the place of a fielder
    - each time a fielder catches a fly ball, he switches positions with the batter

This is a fast-paced game with plenty of opportunities for hitting and fielding the ball. Knowing which outfielder is supposed to be on the batting team next is much less confusing if outfielders are numbered. Using this method, the first base runner to be declared out takes the place of fielder 1, the second to be declared out takes the place of fielder 2, and so forth. The exception to this is when a batter hits a fly ball that is caught. The hitting team is at a slight disadvantage because they have only three hitters. This means someone must produce an extra-base hit to keep the base runners from being out at home base.

Lead-Up Game 6

Purpose: To develop hitting and fielding skills in a small-sided format.

Number of Players: 4
Equipment: 1 safety ball, 2 helmets, 1 bat, 1 batting tee, 1 game marker
Time: 18 to 20 minutes

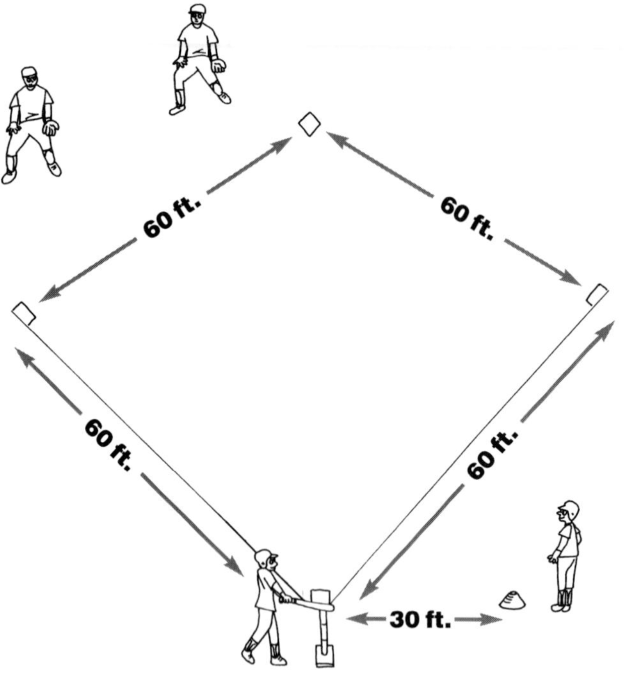

1. Position home plate and bases to make a diamond shape. Bases should be 60 feet apart.
2. Position a designated safety base (game marker) 30 feet behind the batting tee. The batting tee should be situated about 3 feet behind home plate.
3. Divide players into two teams of two players each.
4. Play the game using regular baseball rules with these exceptions:
   - no hitting is allowed to the right side of second base for right-handed hitters and to the left side of second base for left-handed hitters
   - if the hitting team has both players on the bases and no one to hit, they automatically switch roles and become the fielders
5. After 8 runs or 3 outs, switch roles.

This game provides plenty of movement and decision-making opportunities. Among other things, players must decide where the open spaces in which to hit the ball are located and how many bases they can touch after hitting. This game introduces communication between fielders and demonstrates the importance of vision in knowing the correct base for the throw. A large part of the game strategy is finding a way to allow batters the fewest possible bases on each at bat. For example, if the fielders can hold a batter to a single, the next batter must hit the ball far enough for the runner on first to score.

Lead-Up Game 7

Purpose: To develop hitting and fielding skills in a small-sided format.

Number of Players: 8
Equipment: 1 safety ball, 4 helmets, 1 bat, 1 batting tee, 4 game markers
Time: 18 to 20 minutes

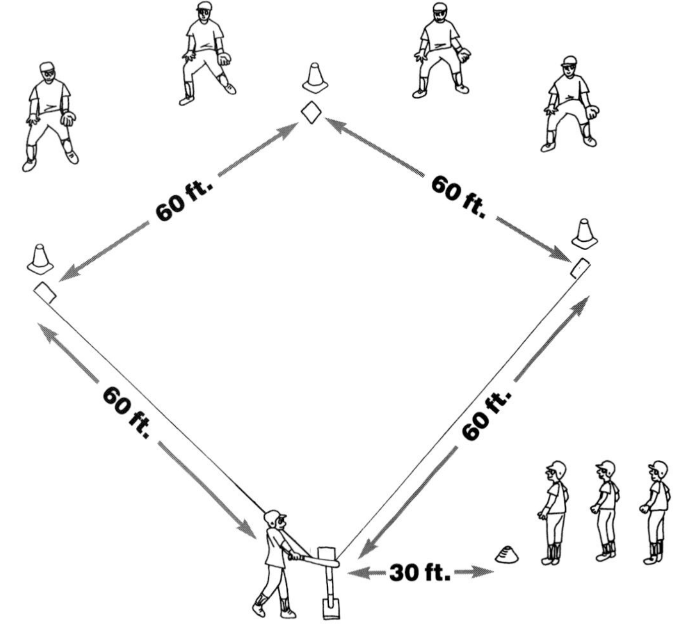

1. Position home plate and bases to make a diamond shape. Bases should be 60 feet apart.
2. Position a designated safety base (game marker) 30 feet behind the batting tee. The batting tee should be situated about 3 feet behind home plate. Position game markers at first, second, and third base.
3. Divide the players into two teams of four.
4. Position the batting team behind the safety base. Place the fielding team in the field.
5. The batter strikes the ball and then runs around all of the bases.
6. The fielding team retrieves the ball and then throws to first base, where the player holding the ball knocks down the game marker positioned there.
7. The first-base player throws to second base, where the player holding the ball knocks down the game marker positioned there.
8. The player covering second base throws the ball to the third-base player, who knocks down the game marker positioned there.
9. If the base runner touches home plate before the team in the field can knock down all three game markers, the runner is safe. If the fielding team can knock down all three game markers before the runner touches home plate, the runner is out.
10. After each hitting team member takes two turns, the teams switch roles.

This game requires movement, communication, and vision by the fielding team. It is particularly valuable in developing the throwing and catching skills needed to execute infield play. Adjust the distance between bases according to the players' skill level.

Lead-Up Game 8

Purpose: To develop hitting and fielding skills in a small-sided format.

Number of Players: 8
Equipment: 1 safety ball, 4 helmets, 1 bat, 1 batting tee, 1 game marker
Time: 18 to 20 minutes

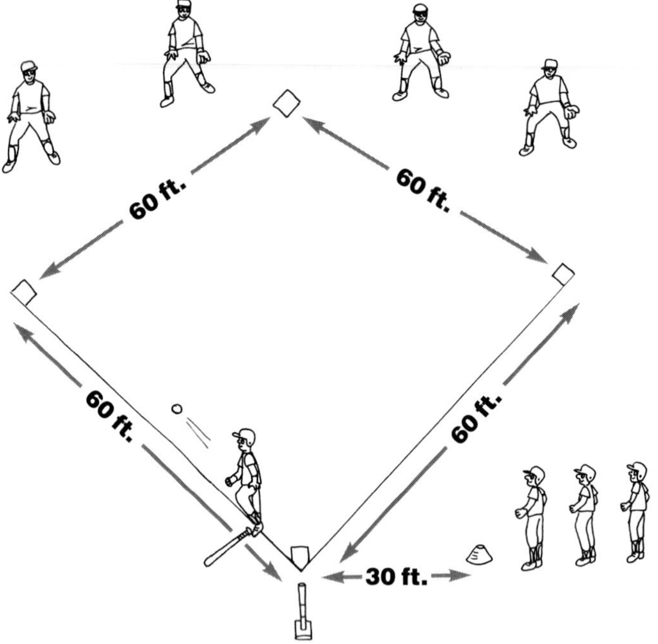

1. Position home plate and bases to make a diamond shape. Bases should be 60 feet apart.
2. Position a designated safety base (game marker) 30 feet behind the batting tee. The batting tee should be situated 3 feet behind home plate.
3. Divide the players into two teams of four players.
4. Position the batting team behind the safety base. Place the fielding team in the field.
5. Play the game using regular baseball rules with these exceptions:
   - if the batter strikes the ball to the left side of second base, he must run to the left (what normally would be third base is now first base); any runner on base must also run to the left if the ball is struck in that direction.
   - if the batter strikes the ball to the right, the batter and all other base runners run to the right.
   - if the next batter strikes the ball the opposite direction as the previous batter, base runners reverse directions.
6. After 8 runs or 3 outs, the teams reverse roles.

Intermediate players love this game. It allows for many opportunities to develop striking and fielding skills. The game also requires players to stay alert concerning baserunning decision making. Much of the game strategy involves where to hit the ball. For example, if several runners are on what would normally be third base (left of home base), the batter wants to hit the ball to the right side so the base runners can touch home base. If the batter decides to hit to the left side, the base runners must run to the left (toward second base instead of home base). This should help develop the concept of a strategy involved with hitting.

Lead-Up Game 9

Purpose: To develop fielding and communication skills for infield play.

Number of Players: 8
Equipment: Tennis balls, safety balls, 4 helmets, 1 bat, 1 tennis racket, 1 batting tee, 6 game markers
Time: 18 to 20 minutes

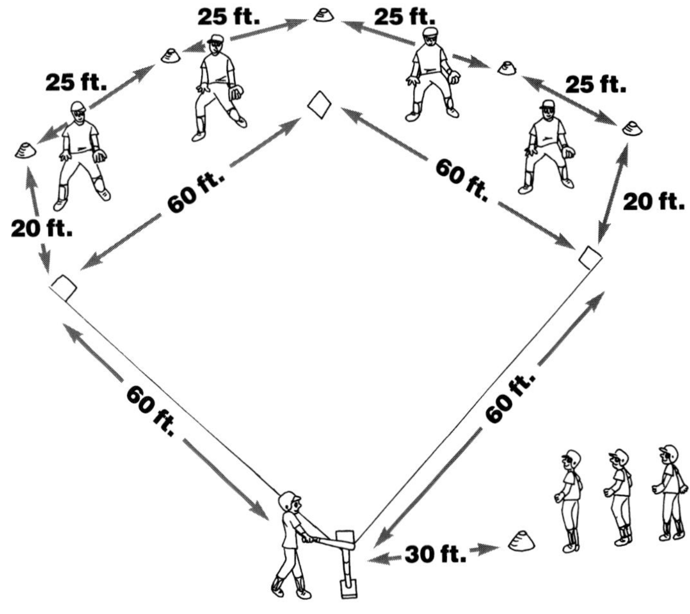

1. Position one home plate and three bases in a diamond shape. Bases should be 60 feet apart.
2. Position a designated safety base (game marker) 30 feet behind the batting tee. The batting tee should be situated about 3 feet behind home plate.
3. Position five other game markers 25 feet apart to form an arc from first to third base, approximately 20 feet behind the bases.
4. Divide players into two teams of four players.
5. Position the batting team behind the safety base. Place the fielding team in the field.
6. The hitters must hit the safety ball off the tee or strike the tennis ball with a racket so that it doesn't pass the arc of the game markers in the air. If the ball does pass the arc in the air, the batter is out.
7. All other regular rules of baseball apply.
8. After 8 runs or 3 outs, the teams reverse roles.

This game provides a great way for infielders to develop the skill of catching fly balls. Using a tennis racket ensures that the balls will be hit high enough in the air to be very challenging to catch. The game also provides numerous double-play situations since the ball isn't allowed to be hit out of the infield in the air.

Lead-Up Game 10

Purpose: To develop game strategies for situational play.

Number of Players: 8
Equipment: 1 safety ball, 4 helmets, 1 bat, 1 batting tee, 1 game marker
Time: 18 to 20 minutes

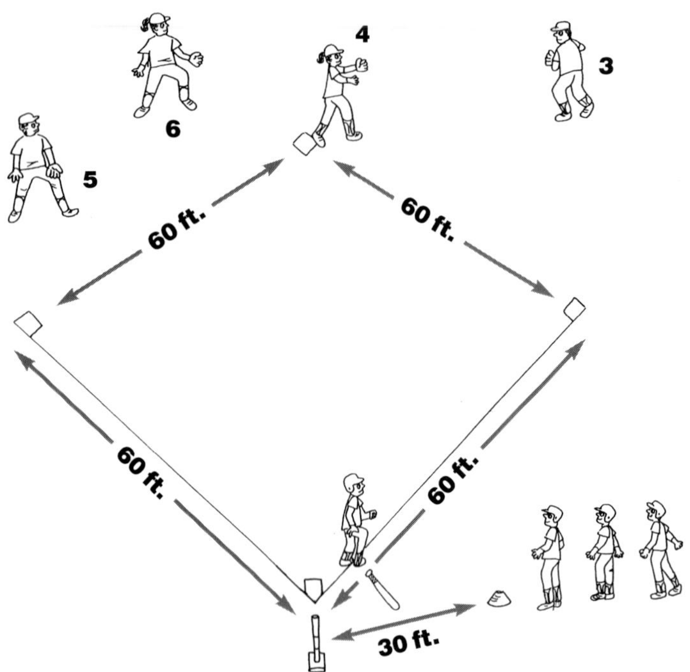

1. Position home plate and bases to make a diamond shape. Bases should be 60 feet apart.
2. Position a designated safety base (game marker) 30 feet behind the batting tee. The batting tee should be situated about 3 feet behind home plate.
3. Divide players into two teams of four players.
4. Position the batting team behind the safety base. Place the fielding team in the field.
5. Players on the hitting team hit the ball and touch as many bases as they can before the fielding team can complete a particular play. For example, in one inning fielders might have to complete a 6-4-3 double play. In this case, the fielders would retrieve the ball from wherever it was hit, throw it to the shortstop (6), who would throw it to the second-base player (4), who would pivot and throw it to the first-base player (3).
6. Each base the hitter touches before the fielding team completes the play counts as 1 run. Base runners may run from third to home to first if fielders are having trouble completing the play.
7. After each player on the hitting team bats twice, the teams switch roles.

In this game, the ball doesn't have to be hit to the shortstop to execute a 6-4-3 double play. It is the fielders' responsibility to retrieve the ball and throw it to a player who has assumed the role of shortstop to start the play. This game offers coaches the opportunity to work on situational play in a gamelike environment. Vary the situations for fielders to include such instances as double-play combinations (3-4-3, 5-4-3, 4-6-3, 5-1-3, etc.); relays from outfield to second, third, and home base; bunting situations; and so forth.

Glossary

Angled-body position: A defensive stance where the fielder places one foot in front of the other and assumes a sideways stance to the hitter.
Backhand: A catch made on the throwing-hand side of the body with the glove positioned so that the fingers are above the thumb.
Backstop: A permanent protective screen behind home plate.
Bailing out: When the hitter steps away from the plate with the front foot to avoid a pitched ball.
Base: Four successive points at the corners of the infield that must be touched by a runner in order to progress to the next and score a run (first, second, third, and home). See also *home plate*.
Baselines: The two lines that run from home plate through first and third base, respectively. They separate fair territory from foul and extend beyond the bases to become the right and left field lines, respectively.
Base path: The running lane for base runners.
Base runner: An offensive player who is on base.
Batter: The player at bat.
Batter's box: A 4-by-6-foot area on the right and left sides of home plate in which the batter must stand when at bat.
Batting tee: A freestanding device that allows batters to hit a stationary ball.
Bunt: An intentionally soft hit made by the batter.
Bunt and run: An offensive strategy used to advance the base runner. The base runner makes sure the ball is not bunted in the air before starting to run.
Calls off: One fielder communicating to another fielder that he is going to field the ball.
Catcher: Position 2, the fielder positioned behind home plate and primarily responsible for receiving pitches.
Center fielder: Position 8, the player positioned in the middle of the outfield.
Choke up: Moving the hands up the bat for more control.
Coach's box: A designated area adjacent to the bases along the first and third baselines from which a coach can direct runners and signal batters.
Covering the base: A reference to what a player does when responsible for plays at a given base.
Crossover step: The technique of pivoting on one foot closest to the direction the player is moving and stepping with the opposite foot across the pivot foot.
Crow-hop: A step-together-step foot action used by fielders to generate more force on their throw.
Cut-off player: A player standing between a thrower and the thrower's target.
Dominant side: The preferred throwing side—for example, right-handers are right-side dominant.
Double: A two-base hit.
Double play: A play in which two outs are recorded on one batted ball.
Double-play depth: A position used by infielders for double-play opportunities. Usually a couple of stops closer to home plate and the fielder's base.
Error: A misplay made by a defensive player resulting in a runner or runners advancing to bases that they otherwise would not have reached.
Extra-base hit: A hit that results in the batter reaching a base other than first base.
Fake bunt and run: When a batter pretends he is going to bunt and then intentionally misses the ball while the base runner(s) advance to the next base.
Fat bat: A plastic bat with a much larger striking surface, which is used to develop striking skills.
First-base player: Position 3, the infielder responsible for plays at first base.
Fleece ball: A very soft ball made from fleece.
Fly ball: A ball hit in the air to the outfield.

Force-out: An out made by tagging a base before it is reached by a runner required to move ahead by the runner behind her.
Foul pop: A ball hit in the air to foul territory.
Fungo: A ball hit for practice fielding by a coach or player who tosses it into the air and hits it.
Fungo bat: A thin, light bat that is easy to control for hitting balls to fielders.
Game marker: A cone-shaped, rubber or plastic piece of equipment used to designate spaces.
Game spot: A flat, round piece of colored rubber used to designate spaces.
Grid: A square or rectangular space designated by game markers for small-group work.
Ground ball: A batted ball that rolls along the ground.
Hitch: When a batter drops his hands before swinging.
Hit-N-Stik: A piece of equipment that looks like a ball attached to a handheld pole and is used to develop striking skills.
Home plate: A 17-inch wide, five-sided slab of whitened rubber at which the batter stands and which must be touched in order to score.
Home run: A four-base hit in which the batter scores a run.
Infielder: A defensive player who plays in the dirt area of the diamond.
J-move: A technique in which a fielder moves to a base using a bending run to receive a throw.
Jump-pivot: A technique of catching the ball, leaving the ground with both feet, and pivoting while in the air.
Left fielder: Position 7, the outfielder covering an area behind third base.
Midline of body: An imaginary line that divides the body into right and left sides.
Nondominant side: The side opposite the preferred throwing side. For right-hand throwers, their left side is their nondominant side.
On-deck circle: The area in which the on-deck batter warms up.
One-hopper: A ground ball hit to a fielder on one bounce.
Out: A play in which a batter or runner is prevented from reaching a base.
Outfielder: A defensive player who is positioned beyond the infield dirt. The three outfield positions are left field, center field, and right field.
Overhand throw: A throw in which the hand is brought back past the ear then extended forward so that the hand is above and slightly to the side of the head.
Pickoff: The act of throwing to an occupied base and getting the runner out without the ball being hit.
Pitcher: Position 1, the fielder designated to deliver the pitch to the batter.
Pitcher's mound: The circular area, usually elevated, from which the pitcher throws to the batter.
Pitcher's rubber: See *rubber*.
Pitchout: The act of the pitcher throwing to the batter's box shoulder high so that the catcher will have an easier opportunity to throw out an advancing runner.
Pivot move: The technique used by a second-base player to turn a double play by stepping on the base with the left foot slightly turned toward first then stepping across the base with the right foot.
Pop-up: A fly ball hit high and short over the infield or short outfield.
Push-off move: The technique used by a second-base player on a double-play ball to touch the base with the left foot and push off to throw to first.
Ready position: The position of an infielder or outfielder before the ball is hit.
Right fielder: Position 9, the outfielder covering an area behind first base.
Rubber: A rectangular whitened rubber slab set in the ground from which the pitcher must be in contact at the start of the motion. The distance from the rubber to home plate on a youth league field is 45 feet, and on a full-size field it is 60 feet, 6 inches.

Run: A score awarded to the offensive team when a runner legally advances to home plate.
Rundown: A defensive strategy for trying to get a runner out who has been caught between bases.
Sacrifice bunt: A bunt in which the batter intentionally gives herself up in order to advance a runner to scoring position.
Safety ball: A commercially available ball that is lighter in weight and has a softer cover to prevent injury.
Safety base: A base located a safe distance behind a batting area at which players can stand when a backstop is unavailable.
Safety net: A net used to restrict the flight of a batted ball or to protect players during practice.
Safety squeeze: An offensive strategy used to score a run in which the batter bunts the ball and the runner on third base, after seeing the ball bunted on the ground, runs toward home base.
Second-base player: Position 4, the infielder positioned to the right of second base.
Short hop: A defensive tactic in which a fielder charges a ball and catches it just as it bounces off the ground.
Shortstop: Position 6, the infielder positioned between second and third base.
Sidearm: A throw in which the ball is released with the throwing arm near perpendicular to the body and horizontal to the ground.
Slide step: A technique used by a fielder to move to a ball by stepping with one foot and sliding the other foot to it.
Station work: Organizing small groups of players in different areas of the field, or stations, to work on different skills at the same time or on the same skill in a different format.
Stealing: In youth league, the act of advancing one base after the pitch has crossed the plate and was not hit by the batter.
Straddle move: A technique used by a second-base player who has plenty of time to turn a double play. The player straddles the base, receives the ball, touches base, and throws in one motion.
Strike zone: When the batter assumes her natural stance, the area over home plate from the bottom of the kneecaps to directly below the batter's armpits.
Suicide bunt: An offensive strategy used to score a run. The runner on third base begins to run toward home as the pitcher's arm is moving forward to release the ball. The batter bunts the ball.
Swing step: A backward step used to change direction when fielding a ball.
T-ball: A game for beginning players in which they strike the ball off a batting tee.
Third-base player: Position 5, the infielder positioned near third base.
Track: When a player follows the path of a ball with his eyes.
Umpire: The ruling official in a baseball game.
Whiffle ball: A plastic ball the same size as a baseball but lighter.
Whiffle bat: A plastic bat used for striking whiffle balls.

Index

Acknowledgments

Thanks to my friend Sharon Mitchell for her countless hours of typing, and to my wife Debra for her support, and for her contribution of the artwork in this book.

About the Author

Jim Garland was a three-time all-conference and all-state college baseball player and was inducted into the Towson University Athletic Hall of Fame in 1985. He has been an elementary physical education teacher for more than three decades, and holds a B.S. and an M.S. in physical education and a doctoral degree in child and youth studies. A former all-conference baseball player for Towson State University, he has played in both the Shenandoah and Cape Cod summer leagues, the top level of amateur baseball. A member of a former All-American Amateur Baseball Champion team, he has pitched batting practice for the Baltimore Orioles and the Cleveland Indians. He has coached youth and high school baseball and conducted many youth baseball cli[illegible] ...a and his sons Casey ar[illegible]

...Mountain Press

...uide,

Guide,

...uide,

...de,

...uide,

...uide,

...uide,